P9-DFS-852

By Deborah Ellis

Looking for X
The Breadwinner
Parvana's Journey
Mud City
Three Wishes: Palestinian and Israeli Children Speak
I Am a Taxi
Sacred Leaf
Jakeman
Off to War: Voices of Soldiers' Children

CHILDREN OF WAR

**High Desert Middle School
Media Center**

CHILDREN
OF WAR

VOICES
OF IRAQI
REFUGEES
DEBORAH ELLIS

GROUNDWOOD BOOKS | HOUSE OF ANANSI PRESS
TORONTO   BERKELEY

Groundwood Books/House of Anansi Press
110 Spadina Avenue, Suite 801
Toronto, Ontario M5V 2K4
or c/o Publishers Group West
1700 Fourth Street, Berkeley, CA 94710

We acknowledge for their financial support of our publishing program the
Canada Council for the Arts, the Government of Canada through the Book
Publishing Industry Development Program (BPIDP) and the Ontario Arts
Council.

 ONTARIO ARTS COUNCIL
CONSEIL DES ARTS DE L'ONTARIO

Library and Archives Canada Cataloguing in Publication
Ellis, Deborah
Children of war : voices of Iraqi refugees / Deborah Ellis.
ISBN 978-0-88899-907-8 (bound).–ISBN 978-0-88899-908-5 (pbk.)
1. Children and war–Iraq–Juvenile literature. 2. Iraq War, 2003-
–Children–Juvenile literature. 3. Refugee children–Iraq–Social
conditions–21st century–Juvenile literature. I. Title.
HV640.5.I75E44 2008   j305.23086'91409567   C2008-905145-9

Design by Michael Solomon
Printed and bound in Canada

To all the families who shared their stories with me.

A refugee's life is never an easy one, but it's especially tough on young people who are robbed of what should be the most formative, promising, and exciting years of their lives. At a time when they should be full of hopes and dreams for the future, they are instead faced with the harsh reality of displacement and privation...

— United Nations High Commissioner for Refugees

As of the end of October, 2008, between 88,373 and 96,466 civilians in Iraq had died violently as a result of the 2003 invasion.*

*Source: www.Iraqbodycount.org. This is a conservative figure. Other estimates are much higher, e.g., www.justforeignpolicy.com estimates the deaths at 1.2 million.

INTRODUCTION

Iraq is a relatively new country, only gaining its independence in 1932. But it is also the site of one of the oldest civilizations in the world. Near Baghdad, the capital, lie the ruins of Babylon, whose hanging gardens were once one of the seven wonders of the world. The oldest written stories in the world, the Gilgamesh cycle, also come from there.

Today Iraq, which is one of the world's important sources of oil, is a war zone. Between 1979 and 2003 the country was ruled by a brutal dictator, Saddam Hussein, who kept its many and various peoples — including Sunni and Shia Muslims, Kurds, Jews, Christians and others — under control by force. He threw his opponents in prison. The Kurds, whose guerrillas wanted independence from Iraq, were bombed with chemical weapons. The majority Shia were attacked, killed and starved by the Sunni-led regime.

Despite the brutality of Saddam's regime, there were positive elements to life in Iraq. Women had equal rights with men and were able to work at any job they were qualified for. There were many great writers, universities and a vibrant intellectual life, though not one that allowed open criticism of the dictator. There was free education for all boys and girls and excellent health care. So at the same time that opponents of the regime were tortured and killed, in general, people who went along with the government led a fairly decent life.

In 1980, Iraq bombed Iran, launching an eight-year war in which more than a million people died. Saddam invaded neighboring Kuwait in 1990, leading to the First Gulf War, in which a coalition led by the United States and sanctioned by the UN drove him back into Iraq.

Saddam used chemical weapons against his enemies and even against his own people, the Kurds. And at one time it appeared that he was trying to develop atomic weapons and other weapons of mass destruction. After the First Gulf War, the United Nations — as part of the peace agreement — was allowed to send in weapons inspectors to search for and destroy these weapons of mass destruction. Saddam did not cooperate with these inspections and made life very difficult for the inspectors, but in the end there was general agreement that the great majority of the weapons, labs and other materials needed to build such weapons had been found, removed and destroyed.

Then came the attacks on the Pentagon and the World Trade Center on September 11, 2001. Although none of the organizers or attackers were from Iraq, the government of George W. Bush was convinced that Iraq was still harboring weapons of mass destruction. They also made the claim, for which no proof has ever been provided, that Saddam Hussein had links to the September 11 attacks. In addition, the Bush government claimed that a war to eliminate Saddam would bring democracy to the Middle East.

Despite world-wide opposition from countries normally allied with the United States, and despite not being able to win support from the United Nations, the United States, Great Britain, Australia and some smaller countries formed what was called the Coalition of the Willing and invaded Iraq in March 2003, bombing Baghdad and launching the Second Gulf War. They did this against the principles embodied in the United Nations Charter. It was, in effect, an illegal war. Saddam Hussein was overthrown quite quickly after massive bombing raids on cities where millions of people lived, and the country was occupied. No weapons of mass destruction were ever found.

The fall of Saddam resulted in new waves of sectarian violence, as various groups inside the country continued to fight for power. At the time of this writing, there were still foreign troops — mainly American forces — in Iraq, and the country had fallen into what some are calling a civil war.

The children in this book are mostly refugees who fled Iraq because of the war and were living in Jordan in the fall of 2007. They represent only a tiny number of those whose lives have been deeply impacted, now and forever, by the American decision to invade their country. Almost 5 million refugees have been displaced by the war. About 3 million are internal refugees — Iraqis who were forced to flee their homes but were unable to cross the border. Many of them are now stuck in remote tent camps without access to schools, health care, electricity, or even food and clean water. Most of the others have fled to nearby countries such as Jordan and Syria, where they face uncertain futures. Others have stayed in Iraq and are trying to rebuild their lives in the towns and cities there. Only a relative handful of Iraqi refugees, even those who worked for the invading army, have been allowed into the countries of the Coalition of the Willing and their NATO allies.

I chose to go to Jordan to collect the interviews for this book simply because the entry process was easier than for Syria. Because English is my only language, most of the interviews were conducted through two interpreters — one associated with the Mandaean community (an ancient religious sect) and one with a group called the Collateral Repair Project, a grassroots organization that provides relief, training, medical care and education to Iraqi refugees.

Time passes quickly. It has been more than seven years since the planes hit the World Trade Center in 2001. It has been nearly six years since the overthrow of Saddam Hussein. Although politicans continue to debate what to do, the war is slipping from the headlines. Yet the children in this book continue to be shaped by these events.

I believe that we can create a world without war. One of the steps we can take is to fully understand the impact of our decisions on the world's most vulnerable — our children.

Deborah Ellis
November, 2008

Turkey

Kurdistan

Aleppo

Mosul

Syria

Kirkuk

Tikrit

Anah Samarra

Lebanon

Syrian
Desert

Baqubah

Ramadi

Damascus

Fallujah Baghd

Israel

Mufrak

Iraq

Zarqa

Euphrates R.

Amman

Jordan

Saudi Arabia

Iraq

Iran

Kut

Tigris R.

Basra

Kuwait

Hibba, 16

The Christian religion is divided into different groups – Catholic, Protestant and many others. Islam is also divided into different groups, including Sunni and Shia.

Saddam Hussein was a Sunni Muslim. When he was in power, the Sunnis in Iraq had more privileges, though more because of tribal allegiances than religious ones. Much of the repression that took place was against the Shia population, although no one was safe.

The Shia groups saw the fall of Saddam Hussein as their chance for revenge. Because there was no fair, workable government in control, many religious and militia groups began to try to take power for themselves. Even nonviolent people who had a long history of brotherhood and sisterhood with Muslims and other religions found themselves swept up in the anger of others.

At the same time that there were religious divisions in Iraq, there were also political divisions. Saddam Hussein was the head of the Ba'ath Party, so many citizens who wanted to advance in industry, government or the academic world joined the party, whether or not they were fans of Saddam.

Hibba's father worked for the Ba'ath government when Saddam was in charge. Like many, he lost his job when the Americans invaded and Paul Bremer, who was in charge of reconstructing Iraq, fired most of the civil service.

Hibba's mother is Sunni. Her father is Shia. Her family has applied to live in the United States.

My mother is Sunni. My father was Shia. This is the way it used to be, before we became divided. Sunni, Shia, no difference, no enemies.

We left Iraq in July of 2003, just a few months after the invasion.

Our father was working with the foreign ministry at the time, so he was part of the government of Saddam Hussein. At the time of all the bombing, he was stationed in Djbouti, at the Iraqi embassy there. We were living with just our mother. I have two older brothers, Saed and Akmed, who are now twenty and nineteen.

The bombing was a terrible time. How would you feel? We were all crowded together in one room. If anything hit our house, we wanted to know where everyone was. We wanted to be able to get to each other. We huddled together and waited to die. Overhead we heard the aircraft, felt the ground shake, heard the world around us exploding.

People watch war in the movies and they think they know what it's like. They don't know. If they knew, they wouldn't allow it to happen. Only very sick, bad people would want to make war.

Paul Bremer came to Iraq and said, "We will make de-Ba'athification." So everyone who ran the country before the Americans came was fired. The Americans didn't understand that people didn't have a lot of choice about joining the Ba'ath Party. You joined if you wanted to get a job in your profession. A lot of good people joined, like my parents.

We managed to stay a few more months in Baghdad until people started making death threats against us. We heard rumors at first, then a group of men in masks came to our house. They told us to get out or we would die.

Even then, we didn't want to leave. Iraq is our home. Why should we leave our home? Then the men came again to our house, and yelled and shot guns at our feet — not to shoot our feet but to scare us, to give us one final message to get out.

This time we left. We joined our father in Amman.

I didn't like leaving Iraq, but at this time I was happy to be in Amman because my father was with us. He was away from us so much with his work that I didn't often get to see him, so to be able to spend so much time with him, even though we were in exile, was wonderful. I was very close to my father. As the youngest of his children I was special in his heart.

In 2006, my father went alone back to Baghdad, leaving us behind in Jordan. Time had passed, and he thought it would be safe. We were running out of money where we were, and he went back to deal with some of our property so that we could pay our bills and keep on eating. He also needed medical treatment, which was too expensive in Jordan. He kept in touch with us by telephone as he moved from one relative's house to another. He thought it was safe, but he wasn't taking any chances.

My oldest brother went back to Baghdad to be with our father, to look out for him and help him.

It was not enough. Our father was kidnapped in May of 2006.

For a while we heard nothing. Then the kidnappers called our relatives and said, "You will find him in the morgue."

My brother went to look, but our father wasn't inside the morgue. He was outside of it, lying on the ground on a rubbish heap on the street. He had a bullet hole in his head.

My brother tried to get back into Jordan, but he wasn't allowed. They said, "You have no legal residency here. You have no papers allowing you to enter." Even if he had papers, they probably still would have said no. Jordan doesn't like to let in young Iraqi men in case they turn out to be terrorists.

Now my brother is in Egypt. We can't go there to visit him because we will not be allowed back into Jordan. And he cannot come here and visit us, so we are separate, and my mother wears widow's black.

My other brother earns a bit of money for the family by jumping from job to job, helping people in the market, cleaning, hauling things, jobs like that. He never works at one place for very long because he's afraid the immigration police will catch him and deport him back to Iraq.

I'd like to be able to finish my schooling and do something about my life, but I don't know how it will be possible to do that the way we live now. The important thing is to try to get the family united again. That won't happen in Jordan.

One of my dreams is to become very educated and very capable and to some day establish some sort of organization to take care of children who have suffered in war. Many have suffered much more than I have, but I have some understanding of what they go through, how they feel their world is taken from them.

We have applied for asylum to the United States. They have accepted us, at least to this stage, so now we have to just wait. It's possible that we may soon be living in America. My mother hopes that my brother can join us there. She says, "If my son is there and we are there and we are all together, that's all we need to be happy," but I don't know.

I don't know how I will feel about living in America, seeing the American flag every day. These are the people who destroyed my country, and they are over there across the ocean living a good life. They destroy things, then they forget about it and have a good supper and watch television. And I will be among them, and will have to get along with them for the good of my family. I don't know if I can do it.

I have nothing in common with American children. How could I? They are raised up with peace and fun and security. They have nothing to worry about. We are raised up with war and fear. It's a big difference. They won't know how to talk to me, and I will have nothing to say to them. Except, maybe, that they should keep their soldiers at home.

But I'll have to find some way to make it work, for the sake of my family. To be together is the important thing, and if we can have that, the rest we will figure out. I imagine we will feel very much like strangers, with a different language, different religion. American soldiers have died in my country, and maybe the Americans we meet will blame my family for those deaths. They won't see us as people. I don't think they will like us, and I don't think we will like them. But at least my family will be together.

To tell you the truth, I try not to think about it. Thinking about it makes me anxious. The Americans cut down trees in my country, and we will be looking at trees still standing in America. The Americans bombed our bridges, and we will be walking across bridges still standing in America. They killed children in my country, and we will be going to school with children who have never known troubles. I don't like to think about it.

Some people think that if you are Iraqi and you are still alive, that your troubles are over. They don't see the other kind of damage. For example, this whole building is full of Iraqis, but we don't talk to each other. There is no trust. The war destroyed that, too.

If I had the power to make the world better, first, there should be peace. To make peace, I would not let anybody make money from selling tanks and guns. If no one could make money that way, they'd have to find some other way to make money. Next, I'd remove all the evil and hatred from the hearts of people, so no one would want to hurt anyone else.

That's what I would do. If I had the power.

R., 18

The area known as Kurdistan has corners in four different countries: Turkey, Iran, Iraq and Syria. It was carved up into today's boundaries by the European powers after World War I. There is oil under the ground in Kurdistan, which was known at the time, although it didn't start flowing until later. The benefits of the oil have not yet managed to trickle down to the Kurdish people.

The Kurds are a separate people from the Arabs or the Turks or the Persians. They have their own language and customs. Traditionally nomadic and tribal, they have had their identity, language and dress forbidden, and they have been forcibly removed from their tribal lands.

Kurdish rebellions have provoked military responses from all four countries. In Iraq, governments before and including that of Saddam Hussein have waged war against Kurdish nationalist groups, assassinating their leaders, destroying hundreds of Iraqi Kurdish villages and herding Kurds into "strategic hamlets," where the Iraqi army could watch over them and control them more easily. Huge numbers of Kurds have been killed with conventional weapons and then, in the late 1980s, with poison gas.

R. is an Iraqi Kurdish teenager now living in Canada.

I am from Kurdistan, in northern Iraq. Terrible things have happened there. I was young when I left, but I still remember, and what I don't remember, my brothers and sisters do.

I'm the youngest in my family. We lived in a village. It was all little villages up there in the mountains. Kurds are not rich people. Most have a few goats or sheep, and they get by. My family lived in that same area for generations, going way, way back.

My father was a soldier in the Iraqi army. He didn't want to be, because he was a Kurd, and his loyalties were with the Kurds, but Iraq was in a war with Iran, and they needed people to fight. The soldiers came in the night and they grabbed my father and other men and said, "Now you are in the army." He didn't have a choice.

I was small, but I remember. We were all crying. I remember that they let him say goodbye to us. He hugged me and said, "I'll come back. I promise."

We didn't see him again for six years. They kept him in the army all that time. No furloughs. He was a prisoner. They don't give furloughs to prisoners!

Things got really bad after he left. Things were bad before, the Iraqi army shooting at us when they weren't shooting at the Iranians, and there were Kurdish militias who were fighting the Iraqis. So that was a regular part of my life.

But it got worse when Saddam stepped up his campaign against my people. People would come flooding through our village on their way out of Iraq, and they would tell stories of gas and of terrible gun battles and dead bodies. I didn't hear those stories myself—or if I did, I didn't understand them—but my older brothers and sister remember, and I know there were a lot of people walking along the road, loaded down with bundles and things.

Pretty soon we joined that long line for the walk to Iran.

I still remember being carried by my mother, being in her arms, and seeing nothing but a long line of people ahead of us with their bundles, and a long line of people behind us. I remember how tired my mother was, and how she sweated from the burden of carrying me. Sometimes I walked beside her, holding her hand, but my legs were short and couldn't go very fast. Plus I think she was really scared that she would lose me, you know, let go of my hand and I'd fall behind in that sea of moving people, and she'd never find me again. So she usually carried me.

I don't know how long we walked. Days, probably, but I don't remember. We crossed over into Iran and ended up in a refugee camp inside the Iranian border.

There were people we knew there, like our neighbors from our home village. We all slept in one tent. It was crowded at the camp, and noisy, and everyone getting into everyone's business because there was no privacy.

My sister was the one who mostly looked after me in the camp because my mother and older brothers were busy trying to find some way to bring in money or food, or were just wandering around looking for things we could use, like wood or scraps to burn. Everyone was cold, everyone was hungry. My mother sold her wedding ring, her extra clothes, anything she could to get food for us.

I think I spent most of my time there trying to escape from my bossy sister! She kept a tight rein on me, because it's dangerous for little kids to wander around refugee camps on their own. They could get hurt, they could get used by a bad crowd, they could pick up bad habits. My sister had a heavy burden. She was only a few years older than me, but she worried about all of us and took care of us. Mom's health was not good. Well, you can imagine.

We were in the refugee camp for four years. That was my life—the tents and the dirt and all the people around. I remember being scared every night, afraid of dying every single night, either from a violent death or from being hungry or cold.

I didn't go to school in the camp. There was no school. My brothers had gone to school when we lived in Iraq, and they have terrible memories of being treated badly there because they were Kurds. They were not allowed to speak Kurdish, only Arabic, and the teachers would beat them when they made mistakes. I don't think they were unhappy at all about missing school while we were in Iran, because school for them was always a violent place.

Finally we came to Canada. We were accepted here as refugees. It was easier for me than the others, because I was still young and had a young brain, so the new language flowed into it quite fast. The others had to struggle harder to learn English, but they had to struggle harder with everything. They are all doing well now, out working in good jobs or in college. But it was rough for a while. My mother still cries about the family she had to leave behind.

We came first. Then my father joined us. He was arrested when he first got here because the government was worried that he might be a terrorist, but they let him go and now he's with us. We've moved around a lot here, trying to find the right place to live where we can be happy.

I was in school the day the planes crashed in New York, on September 11. Kids knew I was from Iraq, and they'd say things, insulting things. I still get called a terrorist. Kids will say, "Don't get him mad or he'll blow up your house."

I keep it together by reminding myself that my mother brought us all here to give us a better life. She would rather have stayed in Kurdistan. Of course, that's her home, that was her parents' home and their parents' home, and back and back. But she brought us here, and I have to prove to her that it was worth it.

I hope I can go back to Kurdistan one day without getting killed. One reason Bush gave for invading Iraq was to stop the killing of the Kurdish people, but Kurds are still being killed. The Americans want oil, and Kurdistan is where the oil is.

If I could talk to American kids, I'd tell them to ask their parents if they believe the war is good, if what they are doing is right. It's one thing if they really believe it, but most people just go along with things without thinking.

When Canadian kids — the ones who have always been here and have had a good life — start complaining to me about the little things that bother them, I just think, "You have no idea."

Michael, 12

The Christian community in Iraq is two thousand years old, and it was about one million strong at the start of the current war.

The chaos that took the place of government after the fall of Saddam brought forward leaders who equated attacks on Christians with attacks on the foreign occupiers, forcing many Christians to flee to Jordan, Syria or wherever they could. Churches have been burned, and Christians have been kidnapped as part of a larger struggle to control areas of the country.

Michael's family belongs to one of the ancient Christian sects of Iraq. They were forced to flee their home and now live in Zarqa, a city northeast of

Amman. Rents are reportedly cheaper in Zarqa than in much of Amman, which is why many Iraqis without means have chosen to settle there. With a population of 700,000, it's the second-largest city in Jordan, and home to a large Palestinian refugee camp.

Michael lives with his mother and younger brother in a few small, tidy rooms, carefully decorated with the few mementos they were able to bring with them from Iraq, and with religious pictures given to them by people in their local church.

I live in Zarqa with my mother and two younger brothers. We came to Jordan two years ago. My father is dead.

My father used to work as a reservations manager in the Sheraton Hotel in Baghdad. I don't think the hotel is there any more. I think it got bombed. I don't know for sure, but I think somebody told me it did.

We are Christian. There have always been Christians in Iraq. We're not like foreigners there. We are a part of Iraq. At the hotel, my father kept a picture of the Virgin Mary on his desk to remind him to think of holy things during his work day. For years he did this, no problem. His manager was also a Christian, and it was fine. Then the Christian manager was fired and a Muslim manager took his place. This new one didn't like the Virgin Mary. He told my father to get rid of the picture. My father didn't want to. I don't know if he was fired or if he quit, but anyway, he was out of a job.

He didn't like to be out of work because he was used to working, and he had to take care of all of us. He couldn't find another job. He became sadder and sadder and sicker and sicker. His stomach hurt and he couldn't eat. The doctor said it was stress, but finally they tested him somehow and said it was cancer. But, like I said, it was too late.

Our home was in Baghdad. We had a very nice house. We weren't there for the bombing, though. We went to Mosul, where my mother thought we would be safer. The planes started attacking two hours after we left, so we just got out in time. Lots of people left if they could, so that George Bush couldn't kill them.

The trip was very hard for my mother. She talks about how hard it was. My father was very sick and he had a tube in his arm attached to a bag that had medicine in it. And my grandmother was with us, but she was sick, too, mostly paralyzed. I am the oldest, but still, I was young, maybe eight, and my two younger brothers had chicken pox. It was a very bad trip.

Mosul wasn't safe, either. There was always gunfire, every night. There were car bombs, too, and a car makes a lot of noise when it explodes.

We spent a lot of time in a church. Maybe we lived there. We were there a lot, anyway, with many other families. At night we would sleep on the floor or on benches, or try to sleep because there were guns all night. Sometimes I'd be so tired I'd forget to be afraid of the guns and just fall asleep anyway.

Our father was getting sicker and sicker, so after a month or so we went to Jordan, but he died in 2004.

My mother said he should be buried in Iraq, because that is our home, and she didn't want his body to be forever in foreign soil. And he was already dead, so George Bush couldn't kill him again. That's when we made the trip with him, wrapped up in sheets in the back of the truck.

We buried him in a graveyard, and then we went back to our house.

There was nothing much left of it. Bombs had hit it. We couldn't even find it at first because bombs had hit the whole neighborhood. Everything was gone. Our house, my friend's house, the house of the people next door and down the street.

Why did they do this? This was my house! This was my street! It wasn't hurting anyone! It was just being a house. The place where I once slept was now rocks and dust and chunks of roof and walls. My things were all broken.

Still, it was ours, so we tried to start living there again, cleaning up the dust and trying to clear up just one room where we could do all our living in. But there was no school, no water, no electricity. Whenever my mother went to the shop, she had to wear hijab because otherwise people would know she was Christian and give her a bad time.

Our lives didn't last like this for long. Very soon, a stranger left a note at our house saying, "Get out or we will kill you." I don't know who left the note. I don't know who wanted us dead.

We left Iraq and came again to Jordan. Now we live in

Zarqa, and we are trying to make our lives here. But everything feels so broken. I miss my father, and I miss my home.

My brothers and I go to school here. I'm the only Iraqi kid in my class. The other students are okay, they're friendly. My best subject is science. We're studying genetics now, and the properties of gas and liquid. It's very interesting. Earlier today we went on a class trip to a park in Amman, with lots of trees and fun things to do.

We don't play much with the neighborhood boys. They're all Jordanian, and they tell us that they don't like Iraqis. My mother worries too much when we leave her sight, like she's afraid we will disappear. So we mostly stay inside, but that means we fight a lot. Especially, I fight with the brother right next to me in age. I used to like him a lot but now he's always plowing into me and throwing things at me.

He wets the bed every night, too. He didn't used to, and he's ten, too old to be doing that. My mother gets him up a lot during the night to go to the bathroom, which wakes me up, so none of us gets much sleep. I try not to tease him about it, because I know he can't help it, but sometimes I do, and that makes me ashamed of myself.

My mother even stopped taking us both to church because she's afraid we'll start fighting in the middle of the service. She takes us one at a time now. I promised myself I won't fight any more, then I do it. Like I said, it makes me ashamed. Our fighting just adds to my mother's unhappiness, so I must find a way to stop it. I see her sitting and staring and looking very unhappy. She used to make fatyr, meat pies, to sell for some money, but the oven broke so she can't do that any more. She forgets all kinds of things, and just sits and stares.

We've been accepted by the UNHCR, and we were supposed to go to Australia, but Australia changed its mind and doesn't want us. So here we sit.

I have nothing in common with American children, except if there is maybe an American child whose father has died, whose house is destroyed, and who is forced to live in a foreign country that doesn't want them. Then he and I would have something to talk about.

I think it would make the world better if people had to fix the things they broke. Like, if someone bombs your house, they couldn't go away and do things they wanted to do until they built you a new house and fixed what they broke.

Sara, 15

In 1990, after Iraq invaded Kuwait, sanctions were imposed on Iraq by countries around the world. Food, medicine and other goods were prevented from going into Iraq, and the country's economy and its people suffered from being unable to engage in full trade with the rest of the world. Because water-treatment plants had been damaged during the First Gulf War, half the Iraqi population did not have access to clean drinking water. Inflation skyrocketed, the education system collapsed and, as Hadani Ditmars wrote in *Dancing in the No-Fly Zone: A Woman's Journey Through Iraq*, "almost overnight, the lives of most Iraqi citizens went from comfortable to desperate." The sanctions continued until 2003, causing hundreds of thousands of deaths, according to UNICEF.

Sara is old enough to remember those years under sanctions. She lives in the Hashimi district of Amman, near the older downtown. There is a shiny new shopping mall nearby. Behind the wide, bright streets of the commercial area are houses full of small apartments that house many Iraqis, including Sara, her two sisters, her mother and a cousin.

I have two sisters. Their names are Heinine, who is fourteen, and Sabine, who is eleven. Our cousin Nahan is also with us. She is the same age as me.

We live now in a small apartment in Jordan. It's very bare, with just mats along the walls, no good furniture. We burn incense a lot because it covers up the smell of damp and worse things. None of us like it here. We are in the Hashimi section of Amman, where a lot of Iraqis live, but we don't spend time with them. It's hard to know who to trust. A lot of people left Iraq for a lot of reasons. Just because we are all here now in Jordan doesn't mean we all like each other.

Our father died seven years ago from sickness. It was harder to get good health care in Iraq in the time of sanctions. I don't know if he would still be alive or not if there were no sanctions. It's something I don't like to think about.

Although we lost his salary when he died, my mother had a good job. Our lives would have been much worse if our mother didn't have a job. She was an accountant in the educational system.

She was also a member of the Ba'ath Party and worked with the Iraqi Women's Union, a non-governmental organization that helped make women's lives easier day-to-day and also encouraged women to participate in the political life of Iraq. It was a very old organization, around for many years.

After the fall of Saddam, militia groups targeted former Ba'ath party members, killing a lot of them. We would hear about the killings, and we worried that our mother might be targeted.

Eventually she did get a death threat, and that's when we left. We were living in our grandparents' house at the time. We gathered together what we could in a hurry, then left quickly and quietly.

For a while, our mother worked here as a housecleaner in the neighborhood, but now she is sick and tired all the time. I'm not really sure how we are surviving now. I think she borrowed money from someone.

We sold some jewelry and dishes, but a lot of Iraqis are trying to sell things in order to live, so we didn't get a good price for them.

Our mother is thinking that if she can get a sewing machine, she can do some tailoring and bring in some money that way. It would be good to see her busy. I think she would be happier if she had something to do that she liked. She'd have less time then to worry about me.

My sisters and I are back in school this year, because Jordan now lets Iraqi children attend for free. My teachers are good, very kind and patient with us. We lost our school year last year because we couldn't afford to pay the fees, so we are behind and have to work hard to catch up.

School feels safe. We can learn, and we have friends and can laugh and have fun. During the war we saw dead bodies in the streets, explosions, terrible things. It helps to be able to laugh and have a bit of a regular life. Both Heinine and I want to be doctors. Sabine hasn't decided yet.

My mother and grandmother want us to wear hijab. They're afraid for us because we have no father or older brother to protect us. They say, "You are young girls, walking around the streets with your heads uncovered. What if you are attacked by some bad Jordanian men? We cannot go to the police. They will send us back to Iraq!" They talk and worry, and sometimes I just get tired of all their worry. This is the one time I have in my life to be young. I don't want to spend it hiding and worried and afraid.

We all miss our homeland. We had friends there, and lives that could have been wonderful.

I think if American girls my age could meet me, they'd like me. If they were friendly, we could go look in the shops and talk about clothes and music. Then they could tell their parents to stop being afraid of Iraqis.

Eva, 17

The United Nations High Commissioner for Refugees (UNHCR) did a trauma survey of Iraqi refugees in Syria that was published in January 2008. According to the survey, 77 percent of the refugees they talked to had been affected by air bombardment, shelling or rocket attacks; 80 percent had witnessed a shooting and 72 percent had witnessed a car bombing; 68 percent had experienced interrogation, harassment or death threats by militias and 16 percent had been tortured. The survey also found that 75 percent knew someone who had been killed, and 89 percent suffered from depression.

Like many Iraqi families, Eva's family has been

living with war for generations. Eva and her family live in a small, dark apartment in Amman. They are Mandaean Sabians, followers of John the Baptist. The word sabia comes from an Aramaic word meaning to be baptized.

The Sabians have had an up-and-down experience in Iraq, sometimes protected by the government and respected by others, sometimes having to hide from persecution. There have been times when certain professions were denied to them, so they took up what trades they could. Many have passed trades like goldsmithing and silversmithing down through generations.

Since the overthrow of Saddam, many Sabian families have been targeted for political reasons, or by criminal gangs, and many have had to flee Iraq.

We came to Jordan on May 5, 2005, after the killing of my father. He was a goldsmith.

My whole life has been war. Really, from the moment I was born. My mother was giving birth to me when a missile hit the hospital. This was during the war with Iran. It was her first time to give birth, so you can imagine how scared she was anyway, and then the missile hitting.

So I came here in war, and there is still war.

We lived in Basra, in the south of Iraq, near the Iranian border, not too far from the sea. My memories of living there are not very good.

We are Mandaean Sabians, and we were the only Sabian family in our area. It was mostly a Shiite community, and children would throw stones at me when I went outside. They also made fun of me because of my teeth. I have had too many health problems since I was born. I wasn't strong like other children. They would laugh at me and the teachers would be mean, too, because it took me longer to learn. I liked to learn, but it took me longer.

I went only as far as the third grade in Iraq. Then the health problems and the teasing got to be too bad. So I left school. I wish there was a way to learn new things here in Jordan, but there is no chance. My mother is a smart woman and could teach me, but she is too busy to spend the time. I try to help her by doing a lot of the cleaning and taking care of the younger children. When I have some quiet time, I like to write down my thoughts. I'm not good at it, but I like to do it.

My mother says that all the bombing that happened while she was carrying me led to my sickness. My head did not look normal when I was born. The bombs brought many chemicals with them, and a lot of children were damaged, like me and even worse.

After the war with Iran came the first war with the Americans. Then came all the years of sanctions, when it was not possible for me to get treatment.

The sanctions meant there was no electricity, not enough food for many people. We were not a rich family. We had a very simple house, and my father worked in someone else's shop. We had no extras to get us through. We were living like ghosts. We tried to stand on our own feet, because we are a proud family, but it was very hard. There was no good food available. Even the bread was bad and dark. The flour was mixed with wood dust and other things to make the wheat stretch farther.

The bombing time was very loud. A bomb fell on our neighbor's house and the whole earth shook. We were scared all the time. We trembled and shook even when the bombing had stopped. There was no time when we could relax because we were always afraid of the next bombing. When we slept, we had nightmares.

The water supply went bad during the bombing. For three months we had no good water to drink. We drank the bad water anyway, because we needed to drink something, and we were always sick with bad stomachs.

When the soldiers came, we didn't talk to them. The younger children were scared of them because of their tanks and helmets and guns. My mother was always warning the younger ones to stay away, but she didn't really need to. They would have stayed away anyway.

Things fell apart soon after the soldiers came. People started turning on each other. We saw lots of people being killed, shot with pistols, dead bodies.

Our father was killed on a trip to Baghdad to buy and sell gold. That was his job. My youngest brother was with him in the car.

We think the killers were watching him in Basra, followed him to Baghdad, then followed him back home. He was killed on the road back to Basra.

My little brother saw the whole thing. It was set up to look like an accident. The killers' car hit my father's car, right on the driver's door. My father was bleeding, and the killers took all the gold out of his car, even the rings off my father's fingers. My father died in the car.

My little brother lost consciousness after the robbing, from fear, I think. The killers shouted at him, threatened him, and he passed out because he was so scared and from the shock of seeing our father killed. He was six years old at the time. Ever since then, he suffers from bad dreams. He keeps drawing the same pictures over and over again — a car full of blood with dead people in it. Even now he'll have times when he'll just cry and cry.

My other brother, Laith, who is now fifteen, refused to believe that our father was dead until my uncles took him and made him look at the body. That's the only way he would accept it. They made him watch the digging of the grave and watch our father be lowered into it. After he realized our father was really dead, he started to become very rough with the family, yelling and being angry all the time.

We have a proverb that goes, "The walls of the house fall when the husband dies." And that is true for us.

The authorities called my mother and said, "There's been an accident. Your husband has been injured in his legs." My uncles went and saw that he was dead. I don't know why the authorities needed to lie to my mother. The killers were never caught.

Before our father was killed, we were preparing to come to Jordan. We got our passports in October of 2004, and he was killed on November 2. We think our father was killed because the killers knew we were planning to leave and they wanted to steal from us before we left. Other Mandaean goldsmiths had been targeted. Muslim goldsmiths were left alone.

With my father gone, people turned their attention to my whole family and started to pressure us to leave. We were threatened because we are Sabia. Under Saddam, we had freedom, all our rights, and our religion was protected. If we had any complaints, we just had to say them, and we would be protected. Before the war, Sunni, Shia, Sabia, Christian, we all lived together and got along. When my father was killed, many Muslim neighbors came to help us.

But there were also many people who treated us badly — not because they were Muslim, but because they were uneducated. Also, the war made everyone a little crazy. Hating people is not part of our culture, but the war is sending people back to the dark ages. It is destroying who we are. Iraqis love sports and literature, and poetry and science, and gardens, all good things. Iraqis don't like all this killing.

Our religion is very important to us. Our prophet is John the Baptist. He was a good person who taught us to love other people. For so many years we lived in Iraq in peace, in our own communities. After the war, attacks came.

My mother's sister's husband was forced to convert to Islam and be part of a terrorist group. After working with this group for a while, he wanted to convert his sons to Islam. Their mother, my aunt, wanted to keep them Mandaean, so she tried to leave the country with them, but he prevented her.

My mother has lived through too many wars. She is an orphan from war, and still managed to get good marks in school, and get a college diploma in commerce. But all her life has been war, like all of my life, and now she is a widow.

Our house here in Amman is just two rooms, plus a hallway and a very poor kitchen. We have to bathe in the kitchen. Our toilet is very bad. The rooms smell all the time of bad things like the toilet. We all have rashes on our skin. The furniture is what we found in the trash along the street. The rugs on the floor are a gift, though. They came from a mosque. They know we are not Muslim but still they helped us, and the cushions are gifts from other Muslims. The American president says Muslims are bad, but so many of them have been good to us.

I try not to think about tomorrow. I try to keep the house clean, and I try to do things that will make the young ones happy for a while, and when I can, I like to try to write and draw pictures that are beautiful. And that is my life.

Bashar, 12

According to the UN Declaration of the Rights of the Child, children have a right to play. Children can find a way to play no matter where they are, but the adult world can certainly make it easier for them by providing safe playgrounds and toys, and creating a world where play is encouraged.

Children who are refugees are often afraid to play. They are afraid of being picked up by police if they lack documentation, being harassed by locals who do not want them in their country, and being in an unsafe place. Sometimes they have to work to help the family, and there is no time for play. Sometimes their homes are so crowded with people that there are not many places to play.

We have come here to Jordan because of all the killing.

My grandmother lives here with us. She has a bullet in
her leg. She was shot, and the bullet went in but it didn't
come out. It's still there. She has an x-ray of her leg and
you can see where the bullet is. It hurts her, and she com-
plains about pain in her bones. But she doesn't complain
too much. She doesn't want to make us sad.

She was shot on her way to Jordan. She was with her
brother and three of my uncles and my aunt. They were
trying to get out of Iraq, and they were stopped along
the road by men with masks who took all their money.
That's when she was shot, because she argued with
them. She said, "Why should you take our money? It's
all we have! Get your own money!" They didn't like that,
and they shot her in the leg, and they also beat up my
aunt. They beat my aunt's face until it was all bruised
and bloody.

Four people were killed on that trip — my grandmother's brother and three of my uncles.

My grandfather was kidnapped in 2003. Some people
took him from his home, and for many years my grandmother didn't know what had happened. There was no
news, so she was always waiting and wondering.

A month ago, they found his body down in the valley
near a Kurdish village. They recognized him from the
clothes he was wearing and from the golden teeth in his

mouth. They couldn't recognize him from his face because he had been dead too long.

Some good people in the village gave him a proper burial and got word to my grandmother. My grandmother cried when she heard the news. We all did.

I told you about the bullet. She also has headaches a lot from the beating they gave her. My grandmother is a very kind woman who doesn't hurt anyone. Why would someone do these things to her? Bad people can do what they want, and good people get punished. The world is wrong.

My family has applied to go to Australia. I think I would like it there. I've seen pictures, and it's very beautiful, with open spaces and rocks, and also with trees and gardens and ocean. I think there are a lot of different people in Australia, too, so if one group doesn't like us, maybe another group will.

Things are not good for us here. People don't like us, maybe because we are Iraqis and we are living here without permission. Many people in Jordan are kind, but some are mean. It may be the same everywhere.

When my brother and I were a bit younger, we were outside our house, walking in the neighborhood. We came across a big wedding celebration. I think it was a wedding. Maybe it was a religious celebration. We stood to watch because it was something to do. Also, there was a lot of food there, and who doesn't like to look at food?

"Go away," some men shouted at us. We didn't leave right away because we weren't bothering anybody. We weren't in the way. We were on the outside looking in.

But they yelled again, "Go away! Get out of here!"

I was smaller, and they were big and loud and angry. I held my brother's hand and should have run away, but I guess I was surprised that they would be so angry at two little kids.

Then two of the men grabbed a pot of very hot water and threw it at us.

It hurt. I got burns on my legs from where it splashed me, and my brother got burns on his back. There are some scars on my face, too, where the water landed.

We ran home, and my parents took us to the Italian hospital in downtown Amman, which is a very kind place for Iraqis.

Something bad happened to my mother and sister, too, when they went out one day. My sister needed glasses for her eyes, to help her to see better. My mother and sister went out together to get the glasses. A group of young men blocked their way and decided to beat them. I don't know why the men did that. Were they bored? I will never do such things when I am a man. I cannot even think of doing such things.

So, from the beating and from the way we live, my mother has high blood pressure, and both she and my sister have nervous problems. They're afraid to go out of the house, and they get very, very sad.

There are eight of us living in two small rooms. We are too crowded, and because we don't feel safe outside, we are in here together too much. We're always on top of each other, and that's fine when we're all getting along, but terrible if we're not. One person waking up in a bad mood soon means we are all in a bad mood, and then it's terrible.

It's not a healthy house, either. My mother cleans and cleans, but it still smells bad from the sewer, and when it's cold and rainy outside, it's cold and damp in the house.

At least I am back in school this year. I want to be an engineer. My sister wants to be a doctor. I don't know if we'll get what we want. Mostly I would like us to not feel so gloomy all the time.

My brother and I have a small courtyard to play in, and there's a wall that divides the courtyard from the street. We have contests to see who can climb over the wall the fastest. I'm bigger, but he's pretty fast.

And my mother likes things to be pretty. We have a sort of a shrub growing in the courtyard that she and my sister and grandmother have decorated with artificial flowers and fake fruit they found in the street. They like to make things look beautiful. My mother also puts pots of daisies and other flowers around to cheer us all up.

I know my parents worry, about money, about what will happen to us, about how to keep us safe. We cannot go to the police when bad things happen to us because we are here illegally, and they could ship us all back to Iraq. We feel we are on our own.

To make the world better, every town and city should have places where only children can go — all children. It doesn't matter if they are Iraqi or Jordanian or what. They could go there and be safe and play all they wanted, and just be happy.

Haythem, 8

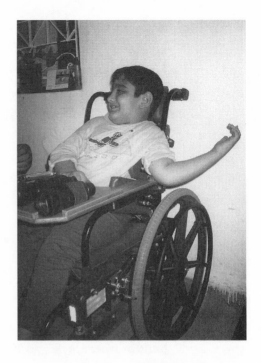

Depleted uranium is waste from nuclear power and from the manufacturing of atomic weapons. It is radioactive, and very dangerous. There are more than a million tonnes of this waste in the world, and it's very expensive and difficult to store. It tends to eat through the containers where it is kept.

One way to get rid of it – or at least get it out of our own backyard – is to sell it cheaply to arms manufacturers, who attach it to conventional weapons to make them stronger and more deadly. During the First Gulf War in 1991, US and British forces sent depleted uranium ammunition into Iraq – ammunition that was toxic not only to the Iraqis, but to the soldiers who fired the weapons as well.

In November 2007 *New Internationalist* reported that between 1990 and 1997, cancer rates in a Basra hospital increased dramatically. Both the children of American soldiers and children in Iraq have been born with birth defects.

Haythem was born with hydrocephalus, a condition that causes fluid to build up in the brain. His condition was made worse in 2005, when four masked gunmen stormed into his home in Baghdad, startling his mother and causing her to drop him. He hit his head on the hard floor. He has had surgery to try to repair the damage, but one side of his head is still badly swollen.

The gunmen kidnapped his uncle and demanded a large sum of money for his release. The family scraped together what they could, paid the ransom and fled the country as soon as the uncle was returned to them.

Haythem's parents suspect that his initial illness came from the weapons that have been used in and against Iraq, but they are unable to prove it. His mother lost two other babies before they were born. When Haythem's uncle was kidnapped, his mother chased the kidnappers out onto the street to try to rescue her brother, but they turned on her and beat her badly. She was seven months pregnant at the time and lost that baby as well.

Haythem lives with his mother, father, uncle and grandmother in a small but sunny apartment on the side of one of Amman's many hills. They have a magnificent view from their courtyard, where Haythem's mother grows pots of herbs and flowers. His father was a soldier and suffers from the trauma of war and from not being able to properly provide for his family.

Haythem likes to read, but he has trouble remembering things, and he has to read them over and over. He can't control the movement of his arms and legs. His father is a silversmith, and he is sad that he will not be able to pass down the art of jewelry making to his son.

The family have been accepted by the UNHCR as refugees, but so far no country has stepped forward to let them in.

I like to play with little cars, and to play games with my father. We set the games up on my tray, and we play.

Sometimes by cousins come over, and we play together. My cousins can understand me when I talk, and they don't laugh at the way I look. The children in the neighborhood can't understand me.

I love to go out into the streets and see what's going on. I like to see people working and playing and doing different things, and I like to look at cars. Sometimes my father takes me out. The hills are very high, and it's hard to push my chair up and down them. People look at me because I look different, and I don't like that.

My mother takes good care of me, and my father plays with me and helps me with my reading. I'd like to go to school, but there is no school for me.

Widian, 14

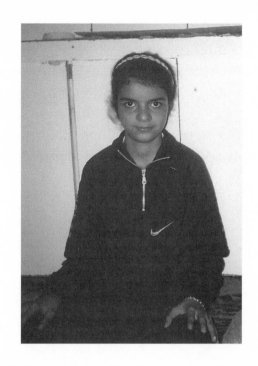

An article in *USA Today* reported that Iraqi psychiatrists are worried about how children there will cope with the long-term effects of being exposed to war and violence. A survey by the Iraqi Ministry of Health found that seventy percent of students in Baghdad are suffering from war trauma and are showing signs of stress like bedwetting and stuttering. Many have had to pass dead bodies on their way to school. Many have repeatedly heard explosions or seen acts of violence on others. There are not enough mental health professionals in Iraq to help them deal with this. "Some of these children are time-bombs," Said al-Hashimi, an Iraqi psychiatrist, said.

Widian and her brother are orphans living with their uncle and his family. They were in Iraq during the heavy bombing. The large extended family lives in three small rooms in the Jebel Amman section – another poverty-stricken area of the city. Mats line the walls of the main room, which are flaky and dark with mold. Their belongings are piled up under blankets.

We live in Amman with my grandmother, two aunts, two uncles and five children, plus my brother and me. The rain comes in when it's raining outside. But at least we are alive.

My father and mother are dead, and so are two of my uncles.

Before the First Gulf War, we were living in Kuwait. Then, when that happened, we moved to Basra, because Kuwait no longer wanted Iraqis in their country.

I have damage in me from the First Gulf War. I wobble when I walk, and I fall down a lot. My muscles and nerves are damaged, they say from the weapons that were used to make Saddam leave Kuwait.

My father was the first one to die. He was captured and murdered. He was tortured to death by electricity. That sort of death leaves marks on your body. When my mother saw him after he died, it was clear what had killed him.

Still, she wanted to be sure, so she had people who knew about such things examine his body and give her papers to say that yes, he had been tortured. She had all these documents with her when she was kidnapped. We heard nothing about her for three months. Then my grandparents got a phone call telling them where to find my mother's body.

My older brother hasn't gone to school for many years because he is afraid of also being kidnapped and killed.

Sometimes I am afraid of that also, and there are other times when I don't care if it happens or not.

We left Iraq in 2004.

When the Americans first came, we all hoped democracy would come, and everyone would be able to live together and be safe. But religious extremists and terrorists took over, and everything became very bad.

We were in Iraq for the heavy bombing. I remember that there was no water or electricity. There were just bombs. It seemed that the big British and American forces were trying to squeeze through our small area. They dropped heavy bombs on us. Not just regular bombs. Heavy bombs. Why are any of us still alive?

We tried to go to sleep early some evenings, thinking that if we managed to fall asleep, we would stay asleep through the bombing. It was foolish thinking. Who could sleep through such things? My head was always cloudy from being scared, and from headaches, and from never getting any rest.

Before the bombing, the people around me, the adults, would talk about how worried they were about what would happen with Saddam no longer in control. They worried that all the tribes and religions would go to war against each other, and that's exactly what happened.

The thing that finally made us leave was when the uncle we were living with got beaten. Gunmen wearing masks over their heads and faces came right into my uncle's house and beat him right there, in his own home. They ordered him to pay them ten thousand dollars or they would come back and kill him and also destroy the house and his shop so that the rest of the family would not be able to eat.

My uncle promised to pay them if they would come back the next day, but before they came back, we gathered what we could carry and came to Jordan.

My brother and I lost so many years of school because of the war, and because of coming to Jordan. This past September was the first time we could go to Jordanian public schools because someone is paying for us to go. But it's not good. They put us into classes that we are way too old for. All the children are smaller than us. It's embarrassing. They put me into the third class, and I am fourteen! I think the school is going to ask me to leave because it's hard for them, too. Then I don't know what I will do.

I like studying and learning things, although it is hard for me. I don't know what I want to be, or how I could ever be what I might want to be.

The thing I most wish for is to have a close friend, a girl my age to play with and who likes to study, like I do. We could learn together and laugh and talk about things that are private between the two of us. That would make me so happy. It would make me feel less alone.

But I am too shy and too weak to make such a friend. I have no chance.

Laith, 11

Kidnapping as a tool of terror became popular in Iraq soon after the fall of Saddam. When Saddam was in power, he would often kidnap and execute political opponents. The kidnappings that have happened since the invasion are sometimes for political purposes, but often are ways for rival gangs to collect money to keep their battles going. Sometimes the kidnappings are for ransom, and the person is returned once the money is paid. Sometimes the kidnapped person is never heard from again.

After the invasion, the Iraqi police force was disbanded, and the American army had no orders to act like police in their place. Groups who wanted to were able to easily take advantage of the situation. Too often, children became the targets.

Laith and his family left Iraq in 2005, after a boy at his school was kidnapped.

My father was a taxi driver in Baghdad. My mother was an agricultural engineer. Neither of them have jobs now. For a while, my father worked at a small booth in the market selling vegetables, but it became too dangerous. The immigration police would show up at the market looking for Iraqis to send back to Iraq. So he stopped working there.

My mother found a way to do a bit of work from home. She makes things like pickles and baskets and candles, then finds a way to sell them. It brings in a bit of money, and that is how we live.

Something happened in Baghdad that made my parents decide to leave.

A child at my school was kidnapped.

It was during the school day. Lots of people were around. The kidnappers wore dark masks over their heads and faces, so it didn't matter that people could see them. They couldn't tell who they were.

They drove up really fast and got out of the car. First they grabbed a girl and tried to stuff her into a car, but she screamed so loud and fought them so much that they dropped her and went after a smaller child, a little boy who was too scared to scream or fight. They put him in the car and drove away. They had these guns and no one could stop them.

Maybe they would have grabbed me or one of my sisters. They didn't really care which child they grabbed. One was the same as another to them. Even now, here in Jordan, when a car pulls up near me on the street, I worry that men with guns will get out and drag me inside, and no one will ever see me again.

The kidnappers went to the boy's family and demanded a lot of money for them to let the boy go. My parents were afraid that if any of us were kidnapped, they would not be able to afford to pay the ransom. So they decided we had all better leave.

I don't know what happened to the boy the kidnappers took. Maybe his parents found the money to pay and he's all right. Maybe he's dead. We left without finding out.

The bombing time was terrible. I was young and didn't understand why the Americans were bombing us. I thought that maybe they didn't know we were there, that we should tell them so that they could drop their bombs where they wouldn't kill anybody.

Those nights were awful. We were stuck in one room with a hundred other people in a place where everyone would go to try to be safe from the explosions. We could hear glass breaking, things blowing up. The whole world would shake. I thought we would all die, and I didn't want to die in that awful room with all those screaming people around.

The bombing ended — the bombing from the sky, that is. Then we saw the American soldiers in the street.

At first they were friendly. They said hello, especially to kids, and we would be friendly back, because kids are friendly people. And sometimes the soldiers gave us sweets, and who doesn't like sweets?

Then they would ask, "Does anyone in your neighborhood have a gun? Tell us who, and we'll give you a whole lot of sweets." Then they would go into the neighborhood and arrest a lot of the people, and the child would get a real bad feeling, a sour feeling. This didn't happen to me, but to kids I know. We would talk about it.

People think children are stupid, that we don't know what's going on. Sometimes we get fooled for a while, when adults lie and pretend to like us, but eventually we figure it out.

Soldiers would sometimes encourage children to surround them, thinking the militias wouldn't attack if it meant killing children, too.

The soldiers being nice didn't last too long. They started being afraid of us. I'd go to or from school, and I'd see the soldiers beating kids, yelling at them and shoving them. Someone told me that they thought the children might be helping the terrorists. Once there was a big explosion near a tank, and soldiers said children had distracted them so they couldn't pay attention to the dangerous people around them. After that they stayed away from us, and we stayed away from them.

The American soldiers did good things, too, though. They didn't just ride around in tanks. They brought supplies to us at school — books and notebooks and pens. And a lot of them did try to be friendly. I want them to see Iraqis as people, so I have to see the Americans as people, too.

After the fall of Saddam, things were quiet for a little

while. Then it started to get dangerous again. People started hating each other, Iraqis hating Iraqis, and lots of killing. Our school was far from our house, and if we were even a little late coming home, my mother would be out looking for us, thinking we had been killed.

I don't like any of my life here in Jordan, except being away from the killing. I want to go home.

I have friends here in school, and they are great, but Jordanian teachers are mean to Iraqi children. They insult us and bully us and don't treat us fairly. There are only two other Iraqis in my class, both girls. One day the teacher said, in front of everyone, "The best Iraqi was Saddam Hussein, and why did you have to come here to make trouble for Jordan? You should all go home."

I've had good teachers here in Jordan, but some of them are just mean.

I try to keep in touch with my friends in Iraq. They called me for a while, but now they've stopped. I think they've forgotten me. I miss them, though. I miss my home, too, and my things. I had to leave nearly all my belongings behind when we came to Jordan.

It's very hard here for my parents. They worry about money and what will happen to us. In Iraq they both had good jobs and made enough money to take care of us. Now they have to beg for everything. They have to go to charities and ask for things. One charity promised us blankets and a heater, but they haven't arrived yet. The weather here is changing. Soon it will be winter, and cold.

If I could talk to American children, I'd say, "Take your soldiers out of my country. I want to go home."

Abinminak, 8

Iraq has a rich history of artists, poets and musicians. Many Iraqi writers and artists have had to continue their work in exile, driven from Iraq by persecution during Saddam's regime, or by the violence of post-Saddam Iraq.

Abinminak's mother is an artist who is hoping to sell her artwork to Americans who are against the war. In Mosul, their home in Iraq, his father taught at an art college. After he put on a play about Abu Ghraib prison and the torture and human rights violations by the Americans, two of the colleagues who worked with him on the play were assassinated. The dean of the college then asked Abinminak's father to leave.

My family and I came to Jordan two years ago, from Ramadi. We left so we would stay alive. I have one sister. She is two years younger than me.

My mother is an artist. She paints beautiful pictures on glass, on ceramics, and on canvas for people to hang on their walls. She did a lot of pieces of art for a woman here in Jordan to sell in her shop, to earn money, but the woman gave them to friends instead of selling them. When my mother asked for her pay, the woman said, "I didn't sell anything, so I have no money to give you." That woman was not honest.

Now my mother has money from CARE to put on an art show. She's busy all the time, making paintings and taking care of us.

I have learned how to paint from my mother. People say I'm very talented. I do a lot of paintings of soldiers shooting tanks and dropping bombs and shooting guns at people, but I also paint happy pictures. I did one I really like of children playing with a butterfly. They keep trying to catch the butterfly, and it keeps flying out of their reach.

My father is an actor. We had to leave Iraq because of a play he was in. We went to Mufrak, in Jordan.

I remember being in my grandparents' house in Ramadi. We were just there, just living, regular life, and American soldiers came in. They just banged right in! They didn't even knock! They were very angry and yelling about something, but they were not yelling in Arabic, so I couldn't understand them. They arrested my uncles. The soldiers beat my uncles and nobody could stop them because they were big and loud and had all these guns.

We had a DVD in the house of people resisting the US army. Someone had made a movie of people trying to attack the Americans. The Americans found it and this made them more angry. I was shaking all over, as if I was cold, but I wasn't cold, and I couldn't stop.

The soldiers came a lot to our neighborhood, a lot to our house. Most of the time they would come in the middle of the night. I stopped sleeping at night so that I could be ready for them. I wouldn't be ready to fight them, because I was too small, but it was less scary if I was already awake when they came. But sometimes they would come in the daytime, too, so I never knew when it was safe to go to sleep.

At night we could hear them running across the rooftops, running from house to house in their big boots. We had a metal door that led from our house to the roof, and one time they broke it with a big crash and came running down our stairs.

Another time we could hear a helicopter coming closer and closer. A helicopter makes a sound like thump-thump, thump-thump, and stirs up the air like a sandstorm. It landed on our roof or on a neighbor's roof. I don't remember for sure. We had put another lock on the metal door to replace the one they broke, but they broke this one, too. I remember the bang-bang-bang when they tried to break the lock.

We all stayed together at night. My parents wanted me close. We wore all our clothes at night, our regular clothes, in case the soldiers came and took us away. We didn't want to be taken away in our pajamas.

I remember one time the soldiers came and they found my aunt praying. They didn't know what she was doing. Maybe they don't pray. They thought she was up to some trouble, so a soldier put a gun to her head. She finished her prayers, then told him to go away.

They came so often that we stopped locking our yard gate, and we left the front door open, too, so they could come in without breaking anything. My father and uncles got tired of fixing things just to have them broken again.

I've seen many people arrested, mostly men and boys — bigger boys than me. I heard from my friends, too, and the friends of my parents, and they said the same things. The women and children would be shoved into one room like the kitchen, and the men would have to lie face down on the floor or the ground. I'd watch sometimes, if my mother or aunts didn't pull me away. It looked like the soldiers were stepping on the men's heads. Some soldiers had the job of yelling and arresting. Other soldiers had the job of breaking furniture and making a mess.

Now we are in Jordan, and no one comes in the night. There are other problems. I hear the problems about money. One of my uncles worked installing satellite dishes for TVs, and his boss wouldn't pay him. He was angry, but what could he do?

I might want to be an actor like my father, but I'll probably be a painter instead. I am also going to be an engineer, because I want to build my family a house that soldiers can't get into.

Things are starting to get a little better for us. My mother is doing an art show for CARE. My father is working on a play for CARE. These things bring in some money, so my parents are happier now and more relaxed. My mother is busy painting, my father is busy acting, and I am busy talking to you. We are a very busy family.

Eman, 18

Eman doesn't talk.

Her father died two weeks ago, from a long illness. She lives with her mother in a small, dark room. Her mother suffers from severe depression, and possibly other mental illnesses.

Her mother collects stale pita bread from shops and restaurants and sells it to Bedouin shepherds, who feed it to their animals.

Eman doesn't go outside. There was no treatment for her in Iraq or in Jordan. Her mother thinks Eman's difficulties are from all the chemicals in the bombs that have been used in the wars. She has no one to help her with Eman's care.

The neighbors walk right into their house and hit

Eman and her mother. When a charity brings them food or blankets, the neighbors sometimes steal from them. "We are poor, too," the neighbors say. "Why doesn't anybody help us?"

It is hard to get a coherent story from Eman's mother. Too many years of too much difficulty have stopped her mind from thinking clearly.

There is a bad smell in the house, and a heavy feeling of damp and dirt.

Rusol, 16, **Sally**, 15, and **Vinn**, 16

The Ahliyyah School for Girls in Amman, Jordan, was founded in 1926. Its big, bright buildings surround a courtyard of volleyball nets and basketball courts. Girls read and giggle in the sun, eating lunches bought at the student-run canteen. The school even has its own forest, and each student is entrusted with a tree to look after while she's there.

Rusol, Sally and Vinn are three of several Iraqi girls who attend the Ahliyyah School, and whose families have the resources to pay the private school fees.

Rusol – I have been in Jordan for five years. We left Iraq one month before the war. We thought something bad was going to happen. Everyone knew the war was coming. We came here first as tourists. We didn't know that we would end up staying so we didn't pack up all our things. We brought very little with us.

I am from Baghdad. My father had a lot of factories in Iraq. My mother was busy at home, taking care of us.

Sally – I came here with my family two years ago. Like Rusol, we didn't know if we would stay. We thought we would just come here as tourists and see what it was like. We decided to stay because the situation in Iraq was very, very bad. Whenever we went off to school, my mother didn't know if she would ever see us again. It was hard for me at first, because I was a stranger here, but when I found friends it became easier.

My family is also from Baghdad, but we went out to Syria during the time of the bombing. We went back to Baghdad for three years after the fall of Saddam. Then we came here.

Our home in Baghdad was a very well-protected place, but all around us, the way between home and school, was very dangerous. It was very hard to go out anywhere, to see friends. You know, I'm a girl, and I want to live my life at this time and do everything. It's hard for me to live in one house between four walls.

That's why we came here, to build a new life without war and without fear.

Vinn – I left Iraq three years ago. During the war and the beginning of the invasion, I was here in Jordan. We were here for a year, then we went back to Baghdad. It was hard for us girls because we had to wear a headscarf every-where. This is not something we were used to, even though we are Muslims. And it was hard for my mother to drive, because the same people who made us cover our heads decided that it was wrong for women to drive! Such thoughts in a forward-thinking country like Iraq. Every time we went anywhere, my father had to drive. If there was a woman driving herself in the car, she would be dead. She would be killed. This is not normal for Iraq. This is backwards.

Sally – We face a very big problem when we travel to another country. They make a big difference between the Iraqi people and other people. It is hard for us to get a visa to go anywhere. We are not dangerous, but still they make it difficult for us.

Rusol – At the same time, we are not planning to stay here in Jordan. Now my father is in Canada, in a place called Winnipeg. He is trying to find work there, and I would like to study there.

Vinn – I will stay in Jordan. I like it here.

Sally – Everybody thinks we Iraqis have a lot of money because our country has oil, but that doesn't mean that we are rich. The American soldiers are sometimes very kind, but there are other strange people in Iraq — not Americans but other nationalities — and they are trying to destroy Iraq now.

Rusol – Saddam Hussein being in power was normal for us. That's how we grew up. We didn't know what was difficult about our lives until we came here and saw another way of doing things. We saw what we were missing. We didn't have internet or satellite TV. When we came to Jordan, we saw these things, and now we are used to them, but under Saddam, it was normal not to have them.

Sally – Maybe we didn't have internet or satellite or mobile phones, but we had security, a good situation, a good life to live. It is not important to have satellite TV. It is more important to have a good life.

Vinn – Everybody was in danger in Iraq. Whenever you left your home, you never knew if you would be alive at the end of your trip. It was hard to feel safe anywhere.

We left behind our house, our books, all our furniture, all our little things that we had gathered in our lives. We had to start here from the beginning.

If I could go back, all I'd really want to get are my pictures — my photos of friends and family and my childhood. Everything else we can get again, or get something like it. But the photos, we can't get. And I can't go home, so I'll never see them.

I think it's hard for American people to see Iraqi people happy.

Sally – It's not the American people, it's the American government. There are a lot of American people who don't like to be killing Iraqis. We have to remember that and not blame the American people for what their government decides.

Rusol – It's important to think of the future, and to work for what we want. I want to study medicine in Canada, to find some nice guy there and get married.

Sally – I also want to be a doctor. I know it's hard, but I will be one.

Vinn – I want to be a pharmacist here in Jordan. I want to live my life in Jordan.

Rusol – If I had the power to make the world better, I would say that we need peace, and to have everyone knowing the culture of everyone else, and having lots of people meet each other and get to know each other, so there will be no fear.

Sally – There should be no difference between Arab people and European people. We should see each other as the same, not one better than the other. An open world, not closed. No borders! No visas! Just people, living.

B., 16

Even those Iraqis who have found safety in Jordan have no reason to believe that safety will last. Jordan, like any nation, has the right to decide who can reside within its borders and under what conditions. Many Jordanians claim that the large influx of Iraqis has pushed down their own wages and raised rents for everyone.

Most Iraqis who are in Jordan now have entered under time-limited visitors' visas. If they are caught staying longer than they have permission for, they are fined, with penalties that grow each day, or they are expelled. If they are caught working without proper permits, they are deported back to Iraq, without the ability to return to Jordan.

Iraqi workers who are cheated by their bosses cannot report this behavior to any authority, since they are not supposed to be working in the first place. Economic hardship forces Iraqis to work illegally, at great risk. They are unable to lead relaxed lives. A single mistake could see them deported back to Iraq. They must take great care not to come to the attention of the authorities. A traffic accident, an argument with neighbors, a problem with a shopkeeper – any of these things could draw the notice of the immigration police and lead to questions about papers and trips back to the border. Iraqis are even afraid to report crimes committed against them, in case that reporting leads to their deportation.

B.'s brother was caught working illegally in Jordan and was sent back to Iraq, which is why B. doesn't want his real name or photo used. He lives with his father and older sister and her baby at the end of an alley. In front of the house is a small walled courtyard of broken concrete. The rooms of the house are small and dark, with water and mold patches on the walls and odd bits of furniture for the family to use.

My brother was caught working here in Jordan, and he was sent back to Iraq. That's why you can't take my picture or use my real name. That's why I never leave the house. I feel that the immigration police are out there watching for me and waiting for me to make a mistake. Then they will grab me. People tell me I am wrong about this, that there are so many Iraqis here the police don't have time to worry about me, that there are lots of others they can catch. To them I say, so where is my brother? And to that they have no answer.

I am almost a man, but I have no work, I have no future. My hair is already turning gray. When I was young, I wanted to be a famous football player. I feel foolish now, for having that dream.

I have been in Jordan with my family for nine years. We live in Zarqa, a crowded, noisy place outside Amman. Our house is a poor house without even a proper ceiling. It's all reeds and we've put plastic under the reeds to keep out the rain and the dust, but it doesn't work that well.

My life was not supposed to be like this. I was supposed to have a different future. My father is a goldsmith. He learned the trade from his father, who learned it from his father, who learned it from his father, back many, many generations. I was supposed to be learning the trade in my father's goldsmith shop in Baghdad, but the shop doesn't exist any more.

When my father was younger he was a very important goldsmith. He went on trips to Bulgaria and other European places, showing people what he could do. The shop was very successful, and we were very rich. We had a beautiful house, many possessions, cars, everything anyone would want. Now look at us! Even the rugs on the floor came from someone else's garbage out in the street.

My father's shop was taken by Saddam because my

father refused to join the Ba'ath Party. Saddam considered him a traitor, took away his shop and threatened to hang him. So we left. We have been in Jordan since before the Americans came. I had to leave school in the sixth grade, and have not been back.

Now my father is very sick. He has diabetes, very bad, and he had to have his leg cut off. They gave him an artificial leg, but he lost a lot of weight, so the leg no longer fits. He usually manages without it, hobbling around on his crutches.

His heart is bad, too. His heart problems became worse when my brother was arrested.

My brother was selling cigarettes in the streets and markets around Zarqa. It wasn't much of a job, but it brought in a little money to help feed us. The Jordanian immigration police grabbed him and said, "Show us your papers!" He didn't have any papers because we're not legal to be in Jordan.

The police brought him back to us in handcuffs and told him to quickly pack a few things. Then they drove him to the Iraq border. We heard from him later that he was met there by American soldiers. He said they treated him well. They let him wash, gave him a bit of money and food. Now he's staying with relatives in Al Kut, two hours from Baghdad. He doesn't do anything there. Just misses us.

My sister lives with us, too. She is older than me and married, although her husband has disappeared. We don't know if he is dead or in prison or what. Maybe the police got him and deported him, or maybe he was just tired of taking care of so many people and went away. We don't know. My sister and her baby live here with us.

We keep to ourselves. We don't want to draw attention.

I don't know where my life will go. Should I go back to Iraq and be with my brother? I hardly know Iraq, and I would have no job there. My only hope is if I can get out of Jordan and start life fresh in a new country, somewhere far away, somewhere new.

I really try not to think. When I think, I am too much reminded of what I've lost, and then it's like I fall into a deep, deep pit, with no way out.

Abbadar, 12

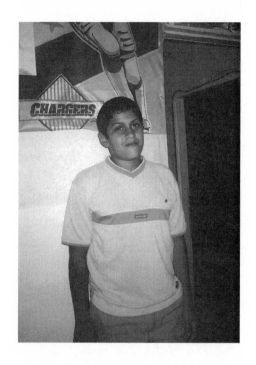

Abbadar lives with his family in an apartment building near a public laundry in Zarqa. His street is fragrant with the scent of detergent. Up a few stories of a narrow, dark staircase is their small apartment. Posters from airlines and sports teams decorate the walls.

The United Nations Declaration of the Rights of the Child states that all children have the right to a nationality, and to documents that protect them. Without these documents, without proof of who they are and where they come from, children are not protected and are denied other rights, such as health care and schooling.

A universal problem for refugees, from no matter

which war or which country, is the loss of papers, the loss of proof of who they are. It makes their struggle that much harder.

My brother was killed eight months ago in Baghdad. He was seventeen years old. Nobody knows who did it, or if they know, they aren't saying. His body was found on a rubbish pile. That's how we know he is dead.

We left both of my older brothers behind in Iraq when we came to Jordan. Jordan doesn't let young Iraqi men into their country. They're afraid young men will become terrorists. They let me in because I am a child. If I were older, they would have said no.

My other brother is still alive in Iraq, but he's homeless. He works in a bakery, and his boss lets him sleep in the storeroom, but that's not like having a real home. He calls us when he can and asks my father to send him money. That makes my father cry, because he doesn't have any money to send.

We live in my sister's house. She is married to a Palestinian, so they can live here and he can work. He sells coffee and tea from a little shop along the street. My sister is twenty-two and has two children. They are very small even for babies, because they don't get the right kind of food. They get sick a lot, too, and there is no medicine.

One of the babies was born in a hospital here in Jordan, but my sister and her husband had no money to pay the hospital fees. They had to sneak out of the hospital with the baby, but they can't get the birth certificate until they pay the bill. Papers are important. You learn that very quickly when you have to leave your country.

I am enrolled in a Jordanian public school. This year they let us into their schools so we can continue our education. We have to be educated so we can be prepared for what life throws at us. I'm a good student. The class I like best is the one where we learn English. If I learn enough English, maybe we can go to America.

It might be better for my father's heart if we went to America. His heart is bad and it got worse when we got the news about my brother's death. He's not able to work, so he has too much time to miss my brothers and to miss our old life.

He has friends who help us out when they can, both Jordanian and Iraqi friends. Like today, someone gave my father some olive oil and some olives for free, as a present. He's very proud to have such good friends.

At one time my father made a very good salary in Iraq. He was a 747 jumbo jet engineer. He's very smart and knows all about how to make airplanes able to fly. But under sanctions, Saddam cut all the salaries, and my father was earning only a little bit of money for doing the same work. It wasn't enough money to live on, so our lives were very hard.

Then he and my mother had a bad feeling that war was coming. It was going to go hard on Iraq, he said. So he and my mother decided we should leave our homeland and come here. It cost them almost all the money they had left for visas for the three of us. We got out just before the bombing started.

My brothers got left behind. Eight months ago, one of them was killed. We don't know who killed him or why. I don't know why they left his body in such a terrible place. I don't know if they killed him as part of the war, or if they just killed him because they were mean anyway. And I don't know if we will ever see my other brother again.

So now, instead of being an important man with an important job, my father stays home and cries a lot because he doesn't see how it will get any better.

Masim, 15

The Iraqi constitution of 1970 included equal rights for women, specifically, their right to vote, attend school, run for office and own property – rights not allowed in many Arab countries. Under Saddam Hussein, women had a harder time maintaining those rights. Saddam tried to tighten his hold on power by making friends with regressive religious leaders, and this also restricted women's mobility and access to jobs. In 1998, to increase jobs for men, the government fired a lot of women working in the civil service. Women were less free to travel abroad, and some co-ed schools were forced to become single-sex.

Since the American invasion, women's rights

have gone on a quick downward spiral. Many have been kidnapped, raped, forbidden to drive and kept from participating in society. Women who had been used to moving around freely were suddenly forced into wearing hijab and staying inside.

Masim lives with her mother, brother and little sister in a nice third-floor apartment in a brand-new building in Amman. Although her mother is educated, she is unable to work in Jordan. She is isolated and at the mercy of her abusive second husband, Masim's stepfather.

We used to live in Baghdad. We never wanted to leave. We stayed all through Saddam, all through the bombing and the invasion, and even through so much death and killing.

We finally had to leave because sectarian militia killed my uncle, because he was a Sunni Muslim from Fallujah, and they threatened to kill the rest of us, too, if we didn't go.

We live in a very lovely new apartment building on the edge of Amman. Amman keeps expanding out into the desert, and we are in one of the new buildings. We have very nice furniture, and when you walk into our apartment, you probably think, what problems could this family have?

I am living here with my brother, Saif, who is seventeen, my mother, my aunt and my half-sister, Meyar, who is five years old.

My father — the father of me and my brother — was a pilot in the Iraqi army. He left our house one day in 1994 and never returned. He was with a special branch of the army that did secret things, and we guess he died doing one of those secret missions. We didn't ask questions. We wouldn't have been given answers anyway.

My mother remarried four years later.

My mother is from Tikrit, from the same tribe as Saddam Hussein. Her new husband — my stepfather — is from a very rich family. He was a friend of my father's and had one wife already. My mother became his second wife. It is not an uncommon custom.

Because Saddam was in power at the time, my stepfather and his family thought that marriage to my mother would be good for their business. Before the invasion, they all treated her very well, and my stepfather treated my brother and me very well, too. My little sister was born, and we all had a good, happy life together.

Then the invasion came, Saddam Hussein was taken from power, and things changed. My mother being from Tikrit was no longer good for my stepfather's business. In fact, having ties to Saddam was now an embarrassment.

My stepfather's brothers, who had been kind and generous to us, now started to speak against my mother. They said my stepfather should get rid of her, that she was a danger to them keeping their lands and fortunes. My stepfather probably would have gotten rid of her, but he really loves his daughter, my little half-sister. That's the only reason he stays married to my mother.

But he stopped being kind to us. He blamed us for all

his problems. He was bitter and nasty, and so was his family.

My mother had nowhere to turn. Her own parents were already dead, so she couldn't go back to them. She has one sister — the aunt who is now living with us. My aunt was married to a man who was related to Saddam Hussein. Her husband was killed. That's what made my stepfather decide we should leave Baghdad.

I will never forget it, the bombing time when the Americans came. Some of the explosions were cars and buildings actually blowing up. Other explosions were just a lot of noise — sound bombs, just to scare us. The people who think up these things are terrible, terrible people.

One night we heard six explosions. They were bombing all the houses around us — one, two, three — the explosions came closer and closer to our house. We were all huddled together waiting to die.

There were six explosions, then a seventh, and then there was a moment of real quiet. Not calm, just silence, like shock. And then all around us was screaming and crying. We went outside and saw all the damage that the bombs had done, and to help the people who had been hurt.

After the bombing time was over, and Saddam was no longer the leader, our lives did not get better. The streets were full of soldiers. The American soldiers came rumbling down our streets in their big Hummers and tanks. They walked around in their big helmets and protective suits. Sometimes they had big black dogs on leashes, and they used the dogs to scare small children. "If you cry, the dogs will attack you," they'd say.

They always had guns pointed at people, at people who had no guns to point back at them. The soldiers broke down people's doors and yelled at people and bothered them.

There was a lot of resistance in our area to the American troops. This wasn't because our area was full of terrorists. This was because people didn't like to see foreign troops trying to control their country. How would Americans or Canadians feel if there were Iraqi troops on your streets, and these Iraqi troops broke down doors and tried to tell you what to do?

But because there was resistance, the American soldiers felt they had to fight back, and their fighting made more resistance. It was a very bad time. There was a lot of killing. My little sister still has nervous fits because of all the dead bodies she saw.

School was closed for a lot of the time. When it reopened, we were driven there in a minibus. Sometimes there would be gunshots at the bus, from the American soldiers and from insurgents. I don't know if they were shooting right at the bus — why would they shoot at a school bus? — or if they were shooting at each other and we just got in the way.

We were at school one day, and some Americans came flying low over the school in an Apache helicopter. Some of the kids yelled at the helicopter and threw rocks at it. The soldiers got mad and tried to land the helicopter in the yard, so the teachers scrambled and got everyone back inside the school. We listened to the helicopter fly away then. Some of the kids cheered, like they had done something great and scared the soldiers away, but they were fools. It's foolish to try to tease people who could easily shoot you and not get into trouble for it.

So now we are in Jordan, and our life is difficult for different reasons.

My stepfather was used to having a very rich, very good life. Losing so much of that has turned him into a very mean man. I think he has psychological problems, too, that make it hard for him to cope. He has a lot of phobias. He is always thinking people are out to get him, or steal from him.

He started hitting my mother, hitting all of us, except my little sister. He said things like, "I will send you all back to Iraq, and when your son is kidnapped, I will not pay the ransom, because he is another man's son. I won't care if he is killed." And he said, "I am feeding you, so you have to do what I say. You are all worthless."

Luckily, he doesn't live with us. He lives with his other family, who are also here in Jordan. But he pays the rent on this apartment, and this furniture belongs to him. He gives my mother a bit of money to look after my little sister, but that's all we have. My mother sold some things that belonged to her only, but that money will soon run out.

My mother is an educated woman, a professional woman. She was working at a good job in Baghdad. Now she has lost all of her self-confidence. She can't work here in Jordan, and she doesn't know how to protect us.

My stepfather comes over whenever he feels like it. He has a key, of course, since he pays the rent. He'll come in and say, "I'm hungry. Go cook for me." And he said that he's paid for the rent for another few months, and when those months are up, he won't pay any more, and we can sleep on the street.

One time he stood out in the street in front of the building and yelled up terrible things at us, insulting things, using bad, terrible curse words.

My brother and I are very good students. My mother had to borrow money to pay our school fees, and she doesn't know how she will pay it back, but she says our education is the most important thing. Without it we will have no hope. My brother is very smart at English and computers. My teacher actually said to my mother, "May God bless you for having such a daughter and for bringing her into my classroom."

So we are all smart people, and should have good futures ahead of us, but so much seems to be beyond our control. My mother doesn't have an independent income, and my stepfather is unstable. We are one tantrum away from being thrown out and having nowhere to live.

I guess I would say to American girls my age the same thing I would say to any girls anywhere. It's the same thing my mother says to me. Be strong and arrange your life so that you can look after yourself, no matter what. Don't rely on a man, even if you fall in love. The man could die or go crazy, and then where would you be?

Abdullah, 13

Fallujah, a city located not far from Baghdad on the Euphrates River, has seen a great deal of fighting that has taken many American and Iraqi lives. During battles in 2004, hundreds of thousands of Iraqis fled the city, and when they returned, many of their homes had been bombed so badly they were no longer fit places to live. There was sewage in the streets from pipes being blown up, no electricity or clean water, and no one to bury the corpses that rotted in empty buildings.

During the battles, US forces fired white phosphorus shells at insurgents. These shells burst into flame on impact, starting fires that can't be put out with water and causing widespread burn injuries among civilians.

Abdullah's father's family comes from Fallujah. He has moved many times since leaving Iraq. His family fled to Jordan when they were threatened by the Mehdi Army, a Shia militia.

We came to Jordan because the Mehdi Army said to my father, "We will kill your son and daughter if you don't leave Iraq." They wanted to kill me because I am Sunni.

My friends were very good in Iraq. Leaving them was difficult. Their names are Athere and Osama. We loved to play football and basketball and go swimming.

I am in grade seven here in Jordan. All the teachers are good, and the other students are also good. No problems.

Baghdad is beautiful, or it used to be. Any place is beautiful when your friends and family are there. I was there during all the bombing. I didn't like it at all, but I was not scared. I was not brave. I was angry. The bombing made me very angry. I didn't know why they were doing this. Why should people be allowed to do such things? I don't understand.

I saw a lot of American soldiers. They were screaming and doing nothing. I mean, they were standing around a lot with their guns, not working. I was a child when all this happened. I don't remember well, because I was in grade one.

I do remember a bit about our life before the Americans came. We had more water and more electricity, and no one was killing other people.

After the Americans came, one of my friends was killed

in the car park of my school. His name was Mohammad. I heard the explosion, and I saw the blood, and my friend was killed. I don't know if it was a car bomb or some other kind of bomb. Does it matter?

When we had to leave Iraq, I left so many of my things behind. The thing I miss most is my computer, and of course my friends and uncles and aunts. I loved playing computer games. My favorite is Tomb Raider. We had to leave all that behind, and bring just a few clothes.

My father is a very brave man. He has moved us around to keep us safe. We moved several times in Baghdad, then to Aleppo, then to Damascus, and now we are here.

My father and his family are from Fallujah. He was there when we were in Damascus. He's a writer, and he writes about Iraq for newspapers and magazines. He's been on Al Jazeera television, shouting about what is going on.

He had a contracting business for twenty years, working with the Japanese and other nations. He had a plastic bag factory, a weaving factory. He did many important things, even worked with the UNHCR. He had to sell one factory. It was worth half a million dollars and he had to sell it for $6,000, because our family was starving because of the war. Someone now will get rich from our misfortune. The building alone was worth a lot of money, but people said, "Either you will sell it to us at this cheap price or we will blow it up." Maybe they had a car bomb. I don't know.

Then the Americans blew up my grandfather's house

in Fallujah. It was a big, good house, and they sent seventeen missiles into it. It still didn't come down, so they blew the rest of it up with TNT.

When fighting started in Fallujah, my father and his friends organized a clinic to take care of wounded people. They even had an ambulance. It wasn't a secret ambulance. It was a very clear ambulance, perfectly marked so everyone would know what it was. It got shot up and destroyed.

They used white phosphorus bombs that set things on fire and make them keep on burning.

That didn't stop him. He saved a lot of families. There were so many bodies in the streets. He got people to a safer place and made a refugee camp for them.

He tried to make an agreement between the resistance and the American army, to stop the fighting. He told the Americans he could get people to stop carrying weapons in the streets and to obey local authorities, if the Americans would agree to stop all the missiles and bombs. He thought he had everyone agreeing, but the next day, the Americans dropped a one-thousand-pound bomb on the city.

So everybody became mad at my father after that. They blamed him for trusting the Americans. He says now that it would be better for him and his family's reputation if he had fought and been killed instead of trying to negotiate with monsters. He means monsters on both sides, but I don't think he really wishes he had picked up a gun. What good would it do us or anyone if he had died?

Now he writes and helps an American group called No

More Victims. They bring children out of Iraq who have been hurt by American soldiers. They find towns in America who will take the children and pay for surgery. I get to meet the children, and the American man, Cole, who helps them. He often stays with us.

I know there can be good people and bad people in every country. All those people in America who help with No More Victims. They don't have to do that. They could be like their government and say, "It's just an Iraqi child. It doesn't matter." But they don't. They try to fix those mistakes. I'm glad there are people like that.

I wish Iraq had no oil. Then people would leave us alone.

I don't know what will happen in the future. So many people have left the country. As long as the American soldiers are there, things will be bad, and people will be killed. I worry that too many people will become used to all this killing and forget that there is a better way to do things.

Jordan is okay, but I don't like it very much. I don't have a good friend here, so I am a little lonely.

I don't know how to make the world better. It's hard to imagine. There is so much that is wrong. I don't know what I would say to American children, but I do know what I would say to George Bush. I'd look him in the face and say, "I hate you."

Shahid, 10

When the Americans overthrew the Iraqi government, they needed to replace it with a new one. To do this, they needed the assistance of the Iraqi people. Many were hired as drivers, interpreters, clerks, guards, and so on.

Those Iraqis who signed on to help the Americans sometimes became targets themselves of people who see the Americans as an occupying force that should be kicked out. Many have been killed, kidnapped or forced to flee.

Sometimes the Americans or British are able to provide some measure of protection for those who work for them. Other times, they are not.

Shahid came to Jordan from Baghdad in March

2005. She lives with her parents and her little brother, Mohammad. Their father worked as an interpreter for the US army, helping the Americans to train new police at the Iraqi police academy. The family is now waiting for permission to live in the United States, although the countries that invaded Iraq have so far taken only a small number of Iraqis, even those like Shahid's father who risked their lives to help them.

I remember Baghdad very well. I miss it. I miss my grandparents, and I miss my friends. I wrote a letter to my best friend in Baghdad, but I can't mail it because there is no mail delivery service to Iraq yet. Here is the letter. Maybe she'll read this book and will know that I am thinking of her.

My dear friend:
I hope your day is full of flowers. I love you and miss you too much. I hope you will forgive me for not sending you a letter sooner. I write you letters, but then I just put them in a bag because I don't know how to send them.

What are you doing now? Do you still play the same games that we played together? Do you remember me and miss me? We had a lot of fun.

I hope that we will come back to you soon, back to our homeland. I have good news. I believe that when I get into the fourth grade, we will go back to Iraq, because in the fourth grade I will learn many new and important things. So, maybe I will see you soon. Inshallah.

My mother says hello to you, and that you should be well, and not cause your mother any worry.

I am out of room, so I say goodbye for now.

Your friend,
Shahid

If we learn of someone going back to Baghdad, maybe they can take my letter and deliver it for me.

The neighborhood where we used to live in Baghdad was very beautiful. It was full of shops, the sort of shops people would want to go to. They could buy dresses and new televisions. They could go to a furniture shop and tell a carpenter what they wanted, and the carpenter would go right to work and make it for them.

And we had the best food in Baghdad, too, in our neighborhood Al Ameed. The best kebab, the best baklava, the best restaurants.

We are Sunni Muslims. My father was a first lieutenant in the Iraqi army, but he hated Saddam. He left the army for medical reasons before the Americans came, and he was very glad to see Saddam gone and be killed.

"Iraq will be better now," he said. "We will have freedom and good laws and proper leaders." He was glad that my brother and I would be growing up in an Iraq without Saddam. He was very disappointed that everything did not work out as he wanted. But even after things started to fall apart, he kept thinking that they would get better. "We shouldn't expect the Americans to fix everything for us," he said. "This is our country. Iraqis have to do the work to make it better."

That's why he volunteered to work with the Americans. He thought he could do good work to bring the country together again. Most Americans can't speak Arabic, so they needed someone to help them communicate.

Our beautiful neighborhood became full of men with guns who shot at people. Bodies would be found on the side of the road and in alleys.

Our father was very secret about working with the Americans, but people found out anyway. Men would stand at the gate to our house and yell at my mother. They'd say, "We know your husband is working for the Americans. We will blow up your car. We will blow up your house. One day you will be surprised because we are coming after you."

There were a lot of men with nothing to do but watch other people and see what they did, and if they saw things they didn't like, they'd shoot or blow things up.

I would hear my parents arguing about it. My mother thought we should get out of Iraq. She was afraid we would be killed. My father thought it was important that we stay, that if all the good people left, Iraq would be lost.

The Americans built a sort of a wall around my neighborhood, so the only people who could come in were the people who lived there. There were fewer killings for a while, I think, but it was like a dead city. The shops closed, and all the things that had made it a good place were not there any more.

The threats kept coming against my father. He went to the Americans and asked them for protection for us, but they had no help to offer.

Finally, he and my mother made the decision that we should leave our country and come to Jordan.

They sold their car, and as many of our belongings as they could. A lot of families were trying to sell things to get money to leave, so they didn't get as much money as they thought they should. I would hear them complaining about it.

We had money when we first came to Jordan, but now it's mostly gone. My father is not allowed to work here, and if he's caught doing a job, he'll be sent back to Iraq, where maybe he will be killed. Sometimes our grandparents send us money from Iraq, and my mother works as a cook. In Iraq, my mother had a degree from a business college. Here she prepares Iraqi dishes for people who have more money than we do, who pay her to cook for weddings or special days.

Her best dish — the one I like best — is koba. It's a rice dish with meat. It's very good.

My brother and I are both in school this year. I'm at the top of my class. My best subject is Arabic. My teachers are all good to me, even though they are Jordanian and I am Iraqi. They don't care about that. They just care that I am a good student and try my best.

I think I would like to be a teacher when I grow up, so that I can be kind to children who have had a hard time. My classmates are friendly, too. There are other Iraqi kids in my class, but there's no difference between us and the Jordanians.

My brother wants to be a painter when he grows up. He wrestles with me a lot because he has all this energy he has to get rid of. He's usually good company, but if he gets to be too much trouble, I just give him a swat. He backs off then. He knows who's boss.

My father did a very good job when he worked with the Americans. They even gave him a certificate saying what a good job he did. It was signed by Mr. Kevin Barry, the instructor at the Baghdad Academy. So they know my father is a good man. We've applied to be allowed to move to the United States. Having that certificate should help us get in.

I'd rather go home, though. My friends are there, and the rest of my family is there. Also, the Americans scare me. They bombed my country, and they made things go very bad. George Bush is scary because he doesn't know about how wonderful the Iraqi people are. I always get scared when I see him on TV, because I am afraid that what he will say will mean more bad news for my country. American children should make their parents elect a kinder president.

Haneen, 10

Two million refugees have left Iraq. Most are in neighboring Jordan and Syria – poor countries that have had little choice but to accommodate the mass influx of refugees.

Meanwhile, countries like Great Britain, Australia, the United States and Canada have shown little willingess to host the millions of Iraqis who sit in limbo in Jordan and Syria and inside Iraq, unable to go back to their old homes and unable to make new lives for themselves.

Haneen and her family are from Baghdad. Their lives have been in upheaval since before the invasion in 2003, and they left Iraq for good in 2007. They are now living in Canada.

We have been in Canada for three months. We were in Iraq until 2007, then we went to Jordan, then we came here. When we lived in Iraq, we lived in Baghdad.

Our mother and father thought we should leave because of all the shooting and bombing. We lived near a police station, and there was shooting around there a lot. One time, the shooting went on and on and it was almost like the sound of rain falling hard.

There was a car blown up in the road by our house, too. It made a very loud noise, and then there was screaming and shouting and sirens. There were always things like that happening.

We left Baghdad before the invasion because my parents thought we'd be safer in Anah, a city in Al Anbar Province. My grandparents had a house there, so we went there, but it wasn't safer. We saw US troops everywhere, in helicopters and in tanks.

Anah is a small city in the desert, with farms around it. There was a lot of bombing. I remember one night when the bombing was going on. We were all together — my parents, my grandparents, my aunts and uncles and cousins. My parents were angry because they thought we would be safe, and everybody was crying except for my little sister and one of my younger cousins. They were laughing, not because they thought it was funny, but because they were so scared. They had lost control of themselves.

We heard all these explosions and everything shook. Glass broke out of the windows. I thought we would all die. But the night passed, and in the morning when it was quiet, we went outside.

All the houses around our house were bombed. But the bombs missed us. Our house was the only one still standing.

I don't remember how long we stayed in Anah, but after a while we went back to Baghdad. Both my mother and father are pharmacists, and they had work to do. We didn't go back to school right away. I forget how long.

It was hard for us because there was no water and no electricity. We saw lots of US soldiers, but we didn't talk to them. We were too scared. A tank came really close to us one day. We saw tanks and soldiers and helicopters all the time. One of the good things about Canada is that there aren't helicopters flying around all the time. I hate that sound.

We did go back to school after a while, but we couldn't go every day. Sometimes there were a lot of shootings or soldiers around, and then we stayed home. On those days Mom would keep us busy playing games and doing things around the house so we wouldn't sit and worry. When the electricity came on we could watch TV, but it never stayed on for long and we never knew when we'd have it.

Then we went to Jordan, and we could go to school there. We learned some English, and played sports and did art. Then we came here.

The war happened because Iraq has oil. And there is a high building somewhere in America that was blown up. They thought Iraq blew it up, so that's why they blew up places in Iraq.

Maybe I'll go back to Iraq some day, if the war ends.

Until then, I'll stay in Canada. We like everything in Canada, especially that there is no bombing. I miss things about Iraq, like my toys and my relatives, but Canada is much easier.

When I grow up, I'm going to be a dentist. My middle sister is going to be a surgeon, and my little sister is going to be a teacher. My parents expect us to work hard, but they want us to have fun, too.

S.W., 19

The journey to safety can be a long and dangerous one. Getting the required papers and being in the right place at the right time are often as much a matter of luck as design. S.W. and her family applied for a visa seven years before they were finally allowed to come to Canada, where her uncle was living and working at two jobs to help support them while they waited for permission to immigrate.

I am old enough that I remember all the changes in my country. Certainly I remember life under Saddam. He was our leader, and I thought he would protect us.

Everyone knew the Americans were coming, but Saddam said we would win the war. Saddam was our government, and we should support our government, like the Americans support their government. We wanted to believe that our government would not let another country come in and take us over.

Even up to the last moments of the war, I was one thousand percent sure that Saddam would do something to save us from the Americans. But it didn't happen.

I am from Baghdad, but we didn't stay in Baghdad during the invasion. My brother has allergies, and one of the things Saddam did was to dig big holes and fill them with oil and set them on fire. The smoke from the burning oil was supposed to confuse the Americans in their fighter planes. I could see the fires from my bedroom window. The air became very hard to breathe, and for my brother it was impossible. So we went to stay with my father's second uncle in Baqubah. We were there for three months and missed the bombing of Baghdad.

My father went back to check on our house almost every day, to make sure it hadn't been bombed or looted. There were people who would go around to homes when no one was there and steal everything.

But just because we didn't see much of the bombing doesn't mean we weren't scared. Staying at my uncle's house was a woman who was pregnant, and she was so scared all the time we thought she would lose the baby.

After three months we went back to Baghdad. It was a city for dead people. Everything was black, it seemed.

There was only the army out on the streets. People stayed in their houses.

Sometimes we had to talk to the American soldiers so we could continue going down the street. I remember one of them who was very polite. We saw him a few times. He said, "Good morning," and "thank you." My mother said if we were nice to them, they would be nice to us. It was safer for us if we were polite.

Even then, with all the Americans in our streets, I thought Saddam was going to do something to let us win the war. But he was quiet for a long time. We didn't know where he was.

I wasn't surprised when he was arrested by the Americans, but I don't think they should have hanged him. Saddam killed a lot of people, and now he's resting in peace. If they had put him in jail for the rest of his life, at least he would have gotten a taste of what he had done to others. A lot of Iraqis don't like that he's resting in peace.

I don't hate him. I don't love him. I have no feelings for him. I'd rather not think about him. Most Arabs can't talk about their governments because their governments don't like other opinions. This is not because of Islam. Islam says there should be lots of opinions. It doesn't say governments should kill their own people.

We went back to our house in Baghdad. It had not been bombed, so we could live there. It was a big house with a beautiful garden, but I just stayed in my room, watching the cars go by on the highway from my bedroom window. It was too dangerous to walk in the streets because you could get killed. I felt like all the plans I had for my future were gone.

We had already applied to Canada because my mother has family here, so we thought we would go to Jordan and wait for the visa. We thought it would come soon. We went into Jordan on a three-month visa and stayed for one year. Every three months we'd have to go to Syria for a day and get another three-month visa for Jordan.

Even though my family said we were safe in Jordan, I was still scared all the time. It didn't help that I couldn't go to school. We couldn't afford it, and Jordan could kick us out at any time. So I had too many days with nothing to do but be scared and worried.

We left Iraq for Jordan on October 23, 2004, and we left Jordan for Iraq on October 23, 2005. Our money had run out.

We stayed in Iraq for six months. I couldn't go back to school because we got there in the middle of the school year and they wouldn't let me enroll.

We got a message that we'd missed our immigration interview so our visa application to Canada was denied. But we never got the message telling us to come to an interview. All those years of hoping to come to Canada, and the hope was gone in a moment.

But we had to keep trying. There was no life for us in Iraq. My mother, little brother and I packed a small bag, enough for three days, and went to Syria to try to get another appointment. My father stayed behind to watch our house. My older brother stayed with him. He had studied at home and had exams to write.

We ended up staying in Syria for three months, but we almost didn't get there.

To cross the border, first you go to the Iraqi border control. They stamped my mother's passport and the driver's passport, but they wouldn't stamp mine. "She should have a man traveling with her," they said. "She is a young girl. She should stay in Iraq, not travel to Syria without a man to protect her."

Mom felt that we had to get to Syria. It was our last chance to get into Canada. She didn't want to take us back to Baghdad. And she couldn't leave me at the border. There's nothing at the border! Just desert! So, what to do?

The driver found a police officer and gave him some money. The police officer went to the border guard, passed the money along, and my passport got stamped.

I was so angry by now. I thought, just hurry and give me my passport so I never have to see your face again.

Then we got to the Syrian border, and the manager there was even worse. He insulted my father for allowing me to travel without a man. He told us to go back to Iraq. He was very mean. If I saw him today, I would kick him.

The whole thing made me very sad. The Syrians used to like us, because Saddam gave them oil, and he gave them electricity even when we didn't have any electricity in Baghdad. The Syrians blame us for not fighting hard enough to keep Saddam in power.

We managed to get our immigration file opened again, gave them lots of ways to contact us for an interview, went back to Iraq to sell all our things, then went back again to Syria.

All this time, we were living on money from my uncle in Canada. He is not a rich man. He was working two jobs, one to support his family, and one to support my family. He opened up a bank account for us in Canada, which meant that we could get credit cards, and we lived on those credit cards and whatever money my uncle could send. By the time we came to Canada, we owed the banks $60,000.

So we sold our things, found good people to look after our house — which belongs to my mother's family, not to us — and went back to Syria for another three months.

Finally, we got a call to go for the immigration interview. We got word to our father, who was still in Iraq, and he headed to Syria. His car was stopped along the highway by a gang of men with guns. He had bags of our stuff in the car with him. They stole all that, and they wanted money. He didn't have any. They got his cellphone and pretended to call my mother and say, "Give us money or we will kill your husband."

They put him in a hole in the ground, and put a machine gun to his head. It must have been a hole they'd used for killing before, because there were other body parts and heads down there.

"We're going to kill you," they kept on saying. Finally, my dad shouted, "Shut the hell up! I don't have any money. My wife doesn't have any money. So go ahead and kill me." Then he said, "But after you kill me, take this bundle of papers to my wife in Syria, if you want to do something good in your life to make up for all the bad."

He didn't act scared, so they thought he was crazy. They stole his passport, but they gave him ten thousand

Iraqi dinars — around five American dollars — and let him get in the car and drive back to Baghdad.

He got back to Baghdad after dark, spent the night at a police checkpoint because he couldn't travel after curfew, then the next day went to see about getting a new passport. That was a whole other long story, but he got it, got to Syria, we had our interview, and the day after we got the visa, we got on a plane and came to Canada.

I like being in Canada. Here, I feel good. Here, no one cares what you do. You can do what you want without being watched by your government or the police or people who are your enemy. Sure, sometimes here people are rude, like they are at times to my mother because she wears hijab, but mostly people are kind and let you live your life.

And I really need to live my life now. I saw things in the last five years that most people don't see even if they live to be ninety. I was put into grade nine when I came here, because I missed so much school and didn't know English, but I'm going into grade twelve in the fall. I'd like to go to college and be an eye doctor. I love so many things — art, music, dancing, guitar, designing, computers and photography.

I want to press a delete button on the last five years of my life, and erase all those unhappy memories.

There should not be any war. If George W. Bush had a problem with Saddam Hussein, they should have both been given a gun, told to take ten steps, then turn and shoot. They could have just killed each other instead of killing and hurting so many other people.

Huthaifa, 19, and Yeman, 13

Although Saddam Hussein was executed on December 30, 2006, Iraq is still torn by ongoing violence, as religious groups and others fight for power. One violent incident can spark a retaliation, and on it goes.

In June 2007, a revered Shia shrine was blown up in Samarra, north of Baghdad, resulting in harsher curfews, retaliation killings of Sunni Muslims, and a new influx of American troops.

Huthaifa and Yeman are brothers who lived in the Ala Dhamiya section of Baghdad – a mostly Sunni area where frequent attacks have taken place since the Samarra bombing. They came to Jordan on July 1, 2006, after a close friend of their father was abducted and killed.

Huthaifa – We left Baghdad just four days after I finished high school. I got a chance to join a college here in Jordan for one year, at Amman University. I was studying in the biomedical engineering department. I studied for only two semesters. Then I had to leave because my family couldn't afford the tuition. Now I have no studying, and no job. It's kind of expensive to live here in Jordan.

I've applied to take several courses here that are offered by NGOs, for capacity-building, photography, media. Also, I play music. I've been playing guitar for five years now. My brother also plays. I'm teaching myself electric guitar. I play mostly progressive rock. Back in Baghdad I had friends who were also into music, and we would get together and play. We weren't a group. We just used to jam together.

Yeman – I am in grade eight, in a private school here, Terra Sancta College. I was just finishing grade six when we left Baghdad.

People were very scared and nervous before the invasion. The American government kept saying scary things, and we were afraid of what they would do.

Huthaifa – There was some talk that America would use atomic weapons in Iraq. They used them against Japan, so we knew they weren't afraid to drop them on people.

There was talk that they might do to Baghdad the same thing they did to Hiroshima.

Before the war, people were used to their lives. Because of sanctions, most people did not have a lot of extra money. They were used to not traveling abroad or doing very adventurous things, just staying in their areas.

Our father had a small video cassette shop, to rent and sell videos, mostly American movies, and music as well. We just went on with our daily lives. We would watch movies from my father's shop. My favorite was *Spawn*. My brother's was *Batman*.

I attended the American-based Baghdad College High School. It is a very good school. Our father went there, too. I made a lot of friends at Baghdad College. They became my best friends, but unfortunately they are still back in Baghdad. I worry about them every day. We contact each other from time to time, but it's not the same.

During the sanctions sometimes we needed medications that we could not get. We needed things for our computers that were not available in the country. After the war, they became available.

Yeman – Before the war, I remember mostly my friends, my school days. We lived in an old neighborhood in the eastern part of Baghdad. The Tigris River wound through it very beautifully. It was a sort of island, the greenest part of Baghdad. A very good place to live.

My favorite thing to do was play computer games. Dead Man's Hand and Grand Theft Auto are the ones I like best. Plus, I play classical guitar.

Huthaifa – There was so much talk on the news of the war coming. We had a satellite dish. Even before the war when it was forbidden, we had one. We watched BBC and CNN and got many different points of view on whether the war would happen or not.

Yeman – It's complicated, the reasons why they wanted to bomb my country. We all know George Bush didn't like Saddam, but it was also that they wanted our oil. I think it was even more reasons than that, reasons we might not know about for a long time.

We heard the bombs and we saw them. Most of the explosions were far from our neighborhood. I think our neighborhood then was one of the safest places in the city, safest from the bombs. We could see the sky light up at night, and of course we heard the noise. Very loud noise. And our window glass got broken from the ground shaking.

When the bombing was happening, the sirens would go off. We were living in our house with eighteen other people. My grandparents and other relatives came to stay with us because their homes were in more dangerous places.

When the sirens went off we would all gather in one small place, because nobody wanted to be alone. The electricity stayed on for the first half of the bombing time, so we would be able to play computer games or watch TV, or listen to music really loud, to drown out the sound of the explosions. When the electricity stopped, we listened to a battery radio, or played cards, and lit candles.

There was also a lot of work to do in the house with all the people living there. We had to get clean water, prepare food, keep things clean.

Even when the bombs were falling, my parents would make jokes and encourage us to make music and play games and tell stories. I think that is the best way to be. Being scared and crying would not have protected us. So we tried to laugh.

Huthaifa – I really thought I would die, but I was ready for it. I felt like an angel, without sins. But later, the war got worse, and then I became afraid.

After the war, the clashes between the militias started happening, and that affected our neighborhood.

Yeman – There was a car bombing at my school one day. I was walking along a corridor with glass all down the side of it. The bomb went off and the glass shattered all around me. I ran away as fast as I could. As the explosion happened, a song came into my mind, "I Disappear," by Metallica. It goes

> Do you bury me when I'm gone?
> Do you teach me while I'm here?
> Just as soon as I belong,
> Then it's time I disappear.

I think it's on the soundtrack for *Mission Impossible II*, with the glass breaking. I felt like I was in a movie.

Huthaifa – I had a lot of thoughts go through my head when we saw Saddam Hussein be executed. Saddam didn't mean anything to us. He did a lot of bad things, but he also did good things. Iraq had a very good education system, free for everyone. Even university was free.

When the Americans came and took Saddam from power, we thought that maybe it is the time for a new, bright Iraq. We were wrong. Many Iraqis would like to have the old days back, because at least then we could have our families together. So many families are separated and spread out far from each other.

For nine to twelve months after Saddam fell, things were kind of getting better. There was killing, but not the same as now. We used to go out and feel safe to stay out until 10 p.m. Then it gradually got earlier and earlier when we felt we needed to be at home.

When the bombing of the shrine in Samarra happened, I was in my last year of high school. It was the most important year in my life because the outcome of the examinations would decide what my future would be. A good average would mean a chance to go to a good university and study medicine or engineering. I had to study a lot. I also went to private lessons. These were held in different areas of Baghdad, so I had to travel around the city. The militias were everywhere in the street. You couldn't predict what was going to happen. We would see a checkpoint and we wouldn't know if it was the real army, or if it was the militia wearing army uniforms, wanting to rob us or kill us.

Yeman – There were many car bombings in our area. We got up every morning to learn that someone else was killed in a brutal way. My friends and I would talk about it. We decided the whole world had gone crazy.

Huthaifa – I remember one of my father's friends predicting this. It was about five days after the fall of Saddam. This friend had a generator, so we could watch TV. I went to his house. He is a doctor and lives in Baghdad with his son, my friend. He said to us, "Don't be very much happy, because things will get worse. One day all of us will have to carry a weapon just to protect ourselves."

After the war, in October of 2003, our father got involved with LIFE, an American-based NGO. LIFE's mission is to rebuild schools, get children school supplies and uniforms, books and bags. There had to be new textbooks, not the ones that were used under Saddam. They do other amazing things, like fixing up the water supply.

Then his colleague at LIFE was abducted and killed. It was a terrible shock for everybody. This was a brilliant man, and a great friend to our father. They killed him the same day they abducted him. It was for sectarian reasons.

Our father decided not to take any more chances with our lives. He sent us out of the country, and he joined us two months later. He stayed on his own in Baghdad to finish up some work.

Yeman – First me, my brother and our mother moved to Syria to stay with my aunt and her children. I thought at first it was going to be a holiday. I didn't know we were leaving forever so I was able to enjoy being in Syria, away from the danger. Then my father called and said we should forget about Baghdad, that we would not be going back.

I cried for three days, because it meant I lost the chance to go to Baghdad College. I wanted to go there so much! It was the only high school in Baghdad that taught only in the English language. It had the most beautiful campus, the biggest in Baghdad, and it has a history of creating leaders. I think even the minister of health for the United Kingdom went there.

Praise God, though, that my father's LIFE office moved from Baghdad to here in Amman. So he has a job, and can continue his work.

Huthaifa – I hope I can continue my studies somehow, here in Amman.

Yeman – In Syria I began to compose music. There is a website called Macjams, where you can meet up with other people creating music all over the world. If you go on it, you can hear some of my music.

Here is the site: www.macjams.com/artist/birdman+ wayne.

Huthaifa – In Baghdad I played guitar for the US army. It was one of those nights the soldiers were going from house to house, searching for weapons. They came to our house at 2:30 in the morning. I was awake, studying for my Arabic final exam. There were five soldiers at the door. I was friendly to them, so they were friendly to me in return. I let them see that we had no weapons, and one of them saw my guitar. His name was Smith, and he was twenty-three, very young. He asked if I would play them a song. He asked in a way that was kind, like he really wanted to hear some music. I played them something from Metallica. You can tell that we both like Metallica. Then he picked up my brother's guitar and we jammed together on "Fade to Black." It was a good moment.

I saw them later, during the day. They asked me to help translate for them with someone. First they asked to search my bag. I was coming home from swimming, so I had my towel and swimsuit in a bag. Then they asked me to help translate. I did, but just for five minutes. Then I got scared that I could be killed for helping them, and I went home.

Yeman – I wish we could use music somehow to stop war. Maybe it sounds silly, but instead of picking up a gun, soldiers should instead pick up a guitar or a saxophone or a trumpet. They could have battles with music, to see who could make the best music. That would make the world much, much better.

Huthaifa – To make the world better, I am planning to be like my father, and find a way to work with an NGO to stop people from suffering.

Yeman – I wish American kids could understand that we have many things in common. Really, we are not different. They don't need to be afraid of us.

Every gun that is made, every warship launched, every rocket fired signifies, in the final sense, a theft from those who hunger and are not fed, those who are cold and are not clothed. This world in arms is not spending money alone. It is spending the sweat of its laborers, the genius of its scientists, the hopes of its children.

— Dwight D. Eisenhower, 1953

Glossary

Abu Ghraib – A prison near Baghdad, known for torture and executions of political prisoners under Saddam. Photos of US soldiers abusing Iraqi prisoners at Abu Ghraib appeared in newspapers around the world. It has been renamed the Baghdad Central Detention Center.

Arabic – A language and a reference to a group of people with roots in the Middle Eastern areas of Iraq, Saudia Arabia and others.

Ba'ath – A political party that stood for Arab unity, socialism and the separation of religion from government. It was formed in the 1950s in the Middle East.

Bedouin – Nomadic Arabs who live in the desert.

Coalition – A collection of diverse groups coming together for a specific purpose.

Democracy – A system of government where citizens choose their leaders and tell them what to do.

Depleted uranium – Radioactive waste product from enriching uranium; it is added to weapons to make them more deadly.

Dictator – A leader who rules by force and does not tolerate dissent.

Dinar – A form of currency in several countries, including Iraq and Jordan.

Guerrilla – An armed fighter who engages in unconventional warfare.

Hijab – A head covering worn by some Muslim women.

Inflation – When the price of goods goes up but the value of money goes down.

Insurgent – Someone who takes up weapons against the official government.

Kurds – An ethnic group from Kurdistan, an area that currently occupies parts of Iraq, Iran, Syria and Turkey.

Mandaean Sabians – Followers of a very old religion that reveres John the Baptist.

Mehdi Army – A Shia Muslim guerrilla army, formed in Iraq after the US invasion in 2003.

Muslim – A follower of the religion of Islam.

NGO – Non-governmental organization.

9/11 – September 11, 2001, the day planes attacked the Pentagon in Washington and the World Trade Center in New York City.

Refugees – People who have to leave their home country because their lives are in danger.

Sanctions – Economic and diplomatic "punishments" one nation can impose on another to try to bring about policy change.

Sectarian – An interpretation of a religion; sectarian violence refers to violence between different branches of the same religion.

Shia – A branch of Islam.

Sunni – A branch of Islam.

Terrorist – Someone who uses violence or the threat of violence to force others to behave in a certain way; generally, terrorism targets civilian populations.

UNICEF – United Nations International Children's Emergency Fund; an agency that helps governments (especially in developing countries) improve the health and education of children and mothers.

Visa – A document allowing someone to enter another country.

White phosphorus – A chemical that can be used to light up areas of a battlefield; it is also mixed with explosives to create weapons that start large fires.

For Further Information

CARE (a humanitarian organization that works around the world with people living in poverty) www.careinternational.org

Caritas (a Catholic humanitarian organization) www.caritas.org

Collateral Repair Project (an American organization that provides assistance to Iraqi refugees and people who need help inside Iraq) www.collateralrepairproject.org

Iraq Body Count (keeps track of confirmed Iraqi civilian deaths due to violence) www.iraqbodycount.org

Iraqi Children's Art Exchange (exchanges art between Iraqi and American children) www.iraqichildrensart.org

Iraqi Red Crescent (Red Crescent is an Islamic relief organization that serves people of all faiths; Iraqi Red Crescent assists Iraqi refugees and those who are internally displaced)

Life for Relief and Development (a Muslim relief organization that assists people around the world) www.lifeusa.org

National Priorities (keeps a tally of the cost of the Iraq war to the American taxpayers) www.nationalpriorities.org

No More Victims (provides medical care in the United States for Iraqi children injured in the war) www.nomorevictims.org

UNHCR (United Nations High Commissioner for Refugees; the UN Refugee Agency formed to protect refugees) www.unhcr.org